JOYZELLE

Joyzelle

Translated by
A. TEIXEIRA DE MATTOS

Monna Vanna

Translated by
ALFRED SUTRO

BY
MAURICE MAETERLINCK

NEW YORK
DODD, MEAD AND COMPANY
1910

CHARACTERS

MERLIN
LANCÉOR, *Merlin's son*
JOYZELLE
ARIELLE, *Merlin's genius, invisible to the others*

SCENE: *Merlin's Island*

ACT I

A Gallery in MERLIN's *Palace*

(MERLIN *is seated near* ARIELLE, *who is sleeping on the steps of a marble staircase. It is night.*)

MERLIN

YOU sleep, my Arielle, you, my inner force, the neglected power which slumbers in every soul and which I alone, till now, awaken at will . . . You sleep, my docile and familiar little fairy, and your hair, straying like a blue mist, invisible to men, mingles with the moon, the perfumes of the night, the rays of the stars, the roses that shed their petals, the spreading sky, to remind us thus that nothing separates us from any existing thing and that our thought does not know where the light begins for which it hopes, nor where the shadow ends which it escapes . . . You are sleeping soundly and, while you sleep, I lose all my knowledge and become like my blind brethren

I

who do not yet know that on this earth there
are as many hidden gods as there are hearts
that throb . . . Alas, I am to them the
genius to be avoided, the wicked sorcerer in
league with their enemies! . . . They have
no enemies, but only subjects who know not
where to find their king . . . They are persuaded that my secret virtue, which is obeyed
by the plants and the stars, by water, stone
and fire and to which the future at times reveals some of its features: they are persuaded
that this new and yet so human virtue is hidden in philtres, in horrible charms, in hellish
herbs and awful signs . . . No, it is in myself, even as it resides in them; it is in you,
my frail Arielle, in you who were once in me
. . . I have taken two or three bolder steps
in the dark . . . I have done a little earlier
what they will do later . . . All things will
be subject to them when they have learnt at
last to revive your goodwill even as I have re-
vived it . . . But it were vain for me to tell
them that you are sleeping here and to point
to your dazzling grace: they would not see
you . . . Each one of them must find you
within himself; each one of them must open

as I do the tomb of his life and come to awake
you as I awake you now . . . [*He bends over*
ARIELLE *and kisses her.*]

ARIELLE

[*Waking.*] Master! . . .

MERLIN

This is the hour, Arielle, when love must
watch . . . I shall often trouble your sleep
in these coming days. . . .

ARIELLE

My sleep was so long that I am always re-
lapsing into it; but I feel stronger and become happier at each new awakening that
your thought imposes on me . . .

MERLIN

Whither are you taking my son and when
shall I see him again? . . .

ARIELLE

I was following him with my eyes in my
attentive dream . . . He is approaching
us . . . He thinks that he is lost; and his

destiny leads him where happiness awaits
him . . .

MERLIN

Will he know me? . . . . It is many
years since the prescribed proof exacted that
we should live as strangers to each other;
and I am eager to be able to embrace him as
I did long ago, when he was a child . . .

ARIELLE

No, fate must be allowed to decide freely;
nor may the proof be falsified by the love of
a father of whose existence he must not
know . . .

MERLIN

But now that Joyzelle is here, close to us;
now that he is coming towards her, does the
future become more clear, can you read further into it? . . .

ARIELLE

[*Gazing upon the sea and the night,
in a sort of trance.*] I read in it what I read
from the first moment . . . Your son's fate
is wholly inscribed within a circle of love. If

he love, if he be loved with a wondrous love, which should be that of all men, but which is becoming so rare that at present it seems to them a dazzling folly; if he love, if he be loved with an ingenuous and yet clear-seeing love, with a love simple and pure and all-powerful as the mountain stream, with an heroic love, yet one that shall be gentler than a flower, with a love which takes all and gives back more than it takes, which never hesitates, which is not deceived; a love which nothing disconcerts and nothing repels, a love which hears and sees naught save a mysterious happiness, invisible to all besides, which perceives it everywhere, in every form and every trial, and which, with a smile, will even commit crime to claim it . . . If he obtain that love, which exists somewhere and is waiting for him in a heart that I seem to have recognised, his life will be longer, fairer, and happier than that of other men. But, if he do not find it before the month is past, for the circle is closing; if Joyzelle's love be not that which the future holds out to him from the high skies; if the flame do not burn its full span, if a regret veil or a doubt obscure

it, then death triumphs and your son is
lost . . .

MERLIN

Ay, for all men the hour of love is an important hour! . . .

ARIELLE

For Lancéor, alas, it is the inexorable hour!
. . . Within these next few days, he will
reach the summit of his life. With groping
hands, he touches happiness and the tomb
. . . He is dependent entirely on the last
steps which he is taking and on the act of the
virgin who is coming to meet him. . . .

MERLIN

And if Joyzelle be not she whom fate
selects? . . .

ARIELLE

Indeed, I fear that the proof which we are
about to attempt is the only one which it
offers; but man must never lose courage in
face of the future . . .

MERLIN

Why attempt the proof if it be uncertain? . . .

6

Joyzelle

ARIELLE

If we do not offer it, fate will offer it; it
is inevitable, but it is left to chance; and
that is why I try to direct its course . . .

MERLIN

And if he love Joyzelle and she do
not love him with the love which fate
demands? . . .

ARIELLE

Then we shall have to intervene more
openly.

MERLIN

How?

ARIELLE

I will try to learn.

MERLIN

Arielle, I conjure you, as this concerns the
dearest being, much dearer than myself;
as I have only one son and he can become
what we well know that I could never be: is
it not possible to make an unexampled, an
almost desperate effort with regard to the
future; to violate time; to snatch from the
years, even were they to revenge themselves

7

upon us two, the secret which they conceal so strictly and which contains much more than our own life and our own happiness? . . .

ARIELLE

No, strive as I may, I can reach no further . . . The future is a world limited by ourselves, in which we discover only that which concerns us and sometimes, by chance, that which interests those whom we love the most . . . I see very clearly all that unfolds itself round Lancéor, until his road meets Joyzelle's road. But around Joyzelle the years are veiled. It is an effulgent veil, a veil of light, but it hides the days as profoundly as a veil of darkness . . . It interrupts life. Then, beyond the veil, I again find happiness and death awaiting him, like two equal, indifferent, inscrutable hosts; and I cannot tell which is the nearer, the more imperious . . . It is not possible for me to know if Joyzelle is the predestined one . . . Everything promises that it is she, but nothing confirms it . . . Her face is stretched towards the coming years . . . and, call to her as I may, with all my might, she does not answer, does not turn her head. Nothing can distract her; and I have never seen her features, which I can only imagine . . . One sign alone is certain: it is that of the very sharp and cruel proofs which she will have to overcome . . . By these proofs alone we shall know her. . . .

MERLIN

And therefore, starting from this point which I can surmount, we must submit to unknown powers, question facts like other men, await their reply and try to conquer them if they threaten harm to those whom we love . . .

ARIELLE

But here they come, in the breaking dawn . . . Let us hasten away; they are coming near . . . Let us leave to their destiny, which is beginning its work, the solitude and the silence which it demands.

[*Exeunt* MERLIN *and* ARIELLE. *A few moments after, while the daylight swiftly increases,* JOYZELLE *and* LANCÉOR *enter from opposite sides and meet.*]

9

Joyzelle

JOYZELLE

[*Stopping, astonished, before* LANCÉOR]:
What are you seeking?

LANCÉOR

I do not know where I am . . . I was
seeking a shelter . . . Who are you?

JOYZELLE

My name is Joyzelle.

LANCÉOR

Joyzelle . . . I am saying the name . . .
It is as caressing as a wing, the breath of a
flower, a whisper of gladness, a ray of light
. . . It describes you completely, it sings in
the heart, it lights the lips . . .

JOYZELLE

'And you, who are you?

LANCÉOR

I no longer myself know who I am . . .
'A few days ago, my name was Lancéor; I
knew where I was and I knew myself . . .
To-day, I seek myself, I grope within myself

and all around me, and I wander in the mist, amid mirages . . .

JOYZELLE

What mist? What mirages? . . . How long have you been on this island? . . .

LANCÉOR

Since yesterday . . .

JOYZELLE

Strange, they did not tell me . . .

LANCÉOR

No one saw me . . . I was wandering on the shore, I was in despair . . .

JOYZELLE

Oh! Why? . . .

LANCÉOR

I was very far from here, I was very far from him, when a letter told me that my old father was dying . . . I took ship at once. We were long at sea; then, in the first port at which the ship put in, I learnt that it was too

late, that my father was no more. . . . I
continued my voyage, at least to be on the
scene of his last thoughts and carry out his
last wishes. . . .

JOYZELLE

Why are you here?

LANCÉOR

Why? I do not know, nor do I know
how. . . . The sea was very still and the sky
was clear. . . . We saw only the water
slumbering in the azure. . . . Suddenly,
without warning, the waves were invaded by
thick blue mists. . . . They rose like a veil,
which clung to our hands, to the rigging, to
our faces. . . . Then the wind blew, our
anchor broke loose and the blind ship, driven
by a current that made her timbers creak,
arrived towards evening in the unknown harbour of this unexpected island. . . . Sad and
disheartened, I landed on the beach; I fell
asleep in a cave overlooking the sea; and,
when I awoke, the fog had lifted and I saw
the ship disappear like a radiant wing on the
horizon of the waves.

12

JOYZELLE

What had happened?

LANCÉOR

I do not know. . . . I would have tried to follow her, but I could find no boat in the harbour. . . . I must wait, therefore, until another vessel passes. . . .

JOYZELLE

That is curious. . . . It is like myself. . . .

LANCÉOR

Like you? . . .

JOYZELLE

Yes, I too came to the island through a thick fog. . . . But I was shipwrecked. . . .

LANCÉOR

When was that? And how? . . . Where do you come from, Joyzelle? . . .

JOYZELLE

I was coming from another island. . . .

Joyzelle

LANCÉOR

Where were you going?

JOYZELLE

Where some one was awaiting me. . . .

LANCÉOR

Who?

JOYZELLE

One whom they had thought right to choose
for me. . . .

LANCÉOR

Were you betrothed? . . .

JOYZELLE

Yes.

LANCÉOR

Do you love him? . . .

JOYZELLE

No.

LANCÉOR

But then? . . .

JOYZELLE

My mother wished it. . . .

Joyzelle

LANCÉOR

Do you intend to obey her?

JOYZELLE

No.

LANCÉOR

Ah, that is well! . . . I like that! . . .
And my father, at the moment of his death,
wished that I also should choose her whom he
had chosen for me. . . . He had his reasons,
very deep and serious reasons, it appears.
. . . And, as he wished it and as he is no
longer alive, I must obey him. . . .

JOYZELLE

Why?

LANCÉOR

We cannot evade the wishes of the dead.

JOYZELLE

Why?

LANCÉOR

They can no longer be altered. . . . **We**
must have pity, we must respect them. . . .

15

Joyzelle

JOYZELLE

No . . .

LANCÉOR

You would not obey? . . .

JOYZELLE

No.

LANCÉOR

Joyzelle! . . . This is horrible! . . .

JOYZELLE

No, the dead are horrible, if they want us
to love those whom we do not love . . .

LANCÉOR

Joyzelle! . . . I am afraid of you . . .

JOYZELLE

I said . . . What did I say? . . . Perhaps I was too quick . . .

LANCÉOR

Joyzelle, your eyes are moist at the
thought of the dead and belie your
words . . .

JOYZELLE

No, it is not for them . . . Perhaps I was harsh . . . And yet, they are wrong.

LANCÉOR

Let us speak no more of the dead . . . You have not told me how your shipwreck . . .

JOYZELLE

We lost our way in a thick fog . . . A fog so thick that it filled our hands, like white feathers . . . The pilot mistook the course . . . He thought he saw a beacon . . . The ship struck upon a hidden reef . . . But no one perished . . . The waves bore me away; and then I saw the blue water glide before my eyes as though I were sinking in a stifling sky . . . I went down and down . . . Then some one caught hold of me and I lost consciousness . . .

LANCÉOR

Who caught hold of you? . . .

JOYZELLE

The lord of this island.

Joyzelle

LANCÉOR

And who is this lord? . . .

JOYZELLE

He is an old man who wanders like a restless shade about this marble palace . . .

LANCÉOR

If I had been there! . . .

JOYZELLE

What would you have done? . . .

LANCÉOR

I should have saved you! . . .

JOYZELLE

Was I not saved? . . .

LANCÉOR

It is not the same thing! . . . You would not have suffered, nothing would have come to you . . . I should have carried you on the crest of the waves . . . Ah, I do not know how . . . Like a cup full of precious pearls, of which not one must be touched by

a shadow; like a flower of the dawn, from
which we fear to shake a single dew-drop
, . . When I think of the dangers which you,
so fair, so fragile, ran among the cruel rocks,
in that old man's arms! . . . What he did
was fine; he did the impossible . . . But it
was not enough . . . How did you reach the
shore at last? . . .

JOYZELLE
I awoke lying on the sands . . . The old
man was there. Then he had me carried
to this palace . . .

LANCÉOR
Is he king of this island? . . .

JOYZELLE
The island is almost desert, one sees none
but a few servants who move about in silence . . . He can have for his subjects only
the trees, the flowers and the happy birds with
which the island seems filled . . .

LANCÉOR
What he did was well done . . .

19

Joyzelle

JOYZELLE

He is good and kind; and he received me
as my father himself could not have received me . . . Yet I do not like him . . .

LANCÉOR

Why?

JOYZELLE

I believe he loves me . . .

LANCÉOR

What! . . . He dares! . . . No, it is not
possible, or else the years no longer have the
weight they should have and reason escapes
us when death draws near . . .

JOYZELLE

And yet I fear it . . . He gave me to understand . . . He is strange and sad . . .
They say he has a son who is very far from
here, who is lost, perhaps . . . He is always
thinking of him . . . When he thinks that
he will see him again, his face lights up, he
. . . Here he is! . . .

[*Enter* MERLIN.]

MERLIN

I was looking for you, Joyzelle . . .
[*Turning to Lancéor, with a threatening
glance.*] As for you, I know who you are
and I know the reasons that have brought
you to this island, the trick of this pretended
shipwreck and the name of the enemy who
sent you . . .

LANCÉOR

Me? . . . But it was a mere accident that
flung me on this coast . . .

MERLIN

Let us waste no phrases.

JOYZELLE

What has he done?

MERLIN

He intended, alas, to do the basest thing
that man can do: to betray kindness, deceive
friendship and sell to the enemy the too
generous host who was going to welcome
him . . .

JOYZELLE

No!

MERLIN

Why? Do you know him?

JOYZELLE

Yes.

MERLIN

Since when?

JOYZELLE

Since I first saw him.

MERLIN

And when did you see him?

JOYZELLE

When he entered this room . . .

MERLIN

That is hardly . . .

JOYZELLE

It is enough.

MERLIN

No, Joyzelle, and soon proofs and facts

will show you that it is not enough and that an honest look, an innocent smile and ingenuous words often conceal more dangerous snares than those of thankless old age or of love that has but little hope . . .

JOYZELLE
What do you mean to do?

MERLIN
I am waiting for the last certainty; and then I shall do what it is lawful and necessary to do to remove all fear of an enemy who would stop at nothing. The pitiless measures which I shall take concern your safety as much as my own; for the same plot surrounds us both and we are united by fate . . . I can tell you no more to-day; have confidence in me; perhaps you already know that your happiness is mine . . .

JOYZELLE
You saved my life, I remember that . . .

MERLIN
You remember it without any kindliness;

but I hope that one day you will do me justice . . . [*To* LANCÉOR] As for you, go! The information which I have received is not open to doubt. When the facts which I fear have confirmed it, I shall act. Meanwhile, you are my prisoner. You will be shown the part of the palace reserved for you. If you go beyond the limits laid down, you become your own judge and pronounce your own sentence. There will be no appeal. Go, my orders are given . . .

LANCÉOR

I obey, but only until you recognise your error. We shall meet soon, Joyzelle . . .

MERLIN

No, bid her farewell; for it is doubtful if you will ever see her again . . . Nevertheless, Joyzelle, chance may bring you again in this man's presence. In that case, fly from him; your life and his depend most strictly on your prompt flight. If I learn that you have seen each other, you are irrevocably lost . . . [*To* LANCÈOR] Do you promise to fly from her?

Joyzelle

LANCÉOR

If her life is at stake, yes.

MERLIN

And you, Joyzelle?

JOYZELLE

No.

CURTAIN

ACT II

(*A wild, neglected garden, full of weeds and
   brambles.   On the right, a very high and
   gloomy wall, pierced by a railed gate.
   JOYZELLE is discovered in the garden,
   alone.*)

JOYZELLE

THIS is the garden which no one
visits.   The sun does not enter here;
the poor wild flowers upon which
men wage war because they are not beautiful
here await death; and the birds are silent.
Here are the violet, which has lost its per-
fume, the trembling, shaking buttercup and
the scarlet poppy, which sheds its petals without ceasing . . . Here are the scabious begging for a little water, the deadly spurge
hiding its green blossoms, the blue campa-
nula silently shaking its useless bells . . . I
know you all, you humble and despised
flowers, so good and so ugly! . . . You could

26

be beautiful; it needs scarce anything: a ray
of happiness, a minute's grace, a bolder
smile to attract the bee . . . But no eye sees
you, no hand sows you, no hand gathers you;
and I have come among you to be also alone
. . . How gloomy everything looks! . . .
The grass is neglected and parched, the leaves
are sick, the old trees dying; and spring itself
and the dew of dawn are afraid lest they
should grow sorrowful in this solitude . . .
[LANCÉOR *appears behind the railed gate.*]

LANCÉOR

Joyzelle! . . .

JOYZELLE

Lancéor! . . .

LANCÉOR

Joyzelle! . . .

JOYZELLE

Go away! . . . Go away! . . . Take
care! . . . It is death if he sees you! . . .

LANCÉOR

He will not see us; he is very far from here.

27

Joyzelle

JOYZELLE

Where is he? . . .

LANCÉOR

I saw him go away. I watched his departure from the top of that tower in which I am a prisoner . . . He is at the other end of the island, near the blue forest that shuts in the horizon . . .

JOYZELLE

But he may return; or some one will tell him . . . Go away, go away, I tell you! . . . Your life is at stake! . . .

LANCÉOR

The palace is deserted; I have gone through the rooms, the gardens and the courts, the long box hedges, the marble staircases . . .

JOYZELLE

Go away, it is only a trap . . . He has a design upon your life; I know it, he said so . . . He suspects that I love you . . . He is only seeking an excuse for what he

would like to do . . . Go away! . . . As
it is, you have done too much . . .

LANCÉOR

No.

JOYZELLE

If you do not go away, then I shall
go . . .

LANCÉOR

If you go, Joyzelle, I shall remain at this
gate until night brings him back to the
palace. . . . He will find me on this for-
bidden threshold . . . I have passed the
limits assigned to me; I have therefore dis-
obeyed him; and I wish him to see it and I
wish him to know it! . . .

JOYZELLE

Lancéor, have pity! I entreat you, Lancéor! . . . You are risking all our happiness! . . . Do not think only of yourself! . . . I will go where you please, if you
will leave that gate! . . . We shall see each
other elsewhere, later, another day . . . We
must choose the time, we must take care, we

must make our preparations . . . See, I am
stretching out my arms to you . . . what
would you have me do? . . . What must I
promise you? . . .

LANCÉOR

Open the gate.

JOYZELLE

No, no, no, I cannot . . .

LANCÉOR

Open, open, Joyzelle, if you would have
me live . . .

JOYZELLE

Why do you wish me to open? . . .

LANCÉOR

I want to see you closer, I want to touch
your hands which I have not yet touched, to
look at you once more as I looked at you on
the first day . . . Open, or I am determined
to be undone; I shall not go away . . .

JOYZELLE

Will you go away then? . . .

Joyzelle

I promise you, Joyzelle . . . As soon as
you open the gate, before a swallow, before
a thought has time to hasten from wherever
it may be to surprise my hand as it touches
yours . . . I beseech you, Joyzelle: this is
too cruel . . . I am standing at this gate
like a blind beggar . . . I can see only your
shadow moving among the leaves . . . These
bars are hateful and hide your face . . .
One look alone, Joyzelle, in which I shall see
you wholly; and then I will go, like a robber
flying with a great treasure dragging noisily
behind him . . . No one will know and we
shall be happy . . .

JOYZELLE

Lancéor, this is terrible! . . . I never
tremble, but I am trembling to-day . . .
Perhaps it means your life; and it already
means mine . . . What is that light which
rises so quickly? . . . It has come to threaten
us, it is going to betray us! . . .

LANCÉOR

No, no, it is the sun rising behind the

wall . . . It is the innocent sun, the good
May sun, which has come to delight us . . .
Open, then, open quickly: each minute that
passes adds its dangers to the dangers which
you fear . . . A single movement, Joyzelle;
a turn of your hand; and you really open the
gates of life to me! [JOYZELLE *turns the
key; the gate opens;* LANCÉOR *crosses the
threshold.*]

LANCÉOR

[*Taking* JOYZELLE *in his arms.*]   Joyzelle! . . .

JOYZELLE

I am here! . . .

LANCÉOR

I hold your hands and your eyes, your hair
and your lips, in the same kiss and at the
same moment, all the gifts of love which I
have never had and all its presence! . . .
My arms are so surprised that they cannot
carry them; and my whole life cannot contain them . . Do not turn away your face,
do not draw back your lips! . . .

32

Joyzelle

It is not to escape you, but to be closer to
you . . .

LANCÉOR
Do not turn your head; do not deprive me
of a shadow of your lashes, a gleam of your
eyes: it is not the hours, but the very minutes
that threaten our happiness . . .

JOYZELLE
I was seeking your smile . . .

LANCÉOR
And your own meets mine in the first kiss
that passes between our lips to unite our destinies . . . It seems to me to-day as though
I had always seen you and always clasped
you and as though I were repeating, in real-
ity, on the threshold of paradise, what I did
on earth when embracing your shadow . . .

JOYZELLE
I used to embrace you at night when I em-
braced my dreams . . .

LANCÉOR
I knew no doubt . . .

33

Joyzelle

I knew no fear . . .

LANCÉOR

And everything is granted me . . .

JOYZELLE

And everything makes me happy! . . .

LANCÉOR

How deep your eyes are and how full of confidence! . . .

JOYZELLE

And how clear are yours and full of certainty! . . .

LANCÉOR

How well I recognise them? . . .

JOYZELLE

And how well I know yours! . . .

LANCÉOR

Your hands rest on my shoulders just as when I lay waiting for them without daring to wake . . .

34

Joyzelle

JOYZELLE

And your arm is round my neck just as it was . . .

LANCÉOR

It was thus that your eyelids used to close at the breath of love . . .

JOYZELLE

And it was thus, too, that the tears came to your eyes when they opened . . .

LANCÉOR

When happiness is so great . . .

JOYZELLE

Unhappiness does not come so long as love binds it . . .

LANCÉOR

Do you love me? . . .

JOYZELLE

Yes . . .

LANCÉOR

Oh, how you said ' yes '! . . . ' Yes ' from the depths of your heart, from the depths of

35

your thought, from the depths of your very
soul! . . . I knew it, perhaps; but it had to
be said; and our kisses themselves did not
count without it . . . Now it is enough,
it will feed my life; all the hatred on earth
could not wipe it away nor thirty years of
distress exhaust it! . . . I am in the light
and the spring overwhelms me! . . . I look
up to the sky and the garden awakens! . . .
Do you hear the birds making the trees sing
and repeating your smile and that wonderful
' yes '; and do you see the rays that caress
your hair like diamonds sparkling among the
flames and the thousands of flowers that bend
over us to surprise in our eyes the mystery of
a love which they did not know? . . .

JOYZELLE

[*Opening her eyes.*] There was nothing
here but poor, dead flowers . . .

> [*She looks around her, stupefied; for,
> since Lancéor's entrance, without their
> noticing it, the gloomy garden has
> become gradually transfigured by
> magic. The wild plants, the weeds
> that poisoned it, have grown, and*

*each, according to its kind, has in-
creased its flowers, blossoming to a
prodigious size. The puny bindweed
has become a powerful creeper, whose
wonderful blossoms engarland the
trees weighed down with ripe fruits
and peopled with marvellous birds.
The white pimpernel is now a tall
shrub of a warm and tender green,
with bursting flowers larger than lilies.
The pale scabious has lengthened its
stalks, from which spring tufts like
mauve heliotrope. . . . Butterflies flit
to and fro, the bees hum, the birds
sing, the fruits swing and fall, the
light streams down. The perspective
of the garden has become infinitely
extended; and the audience now sees,
to the right, a marble basin, half-
hidden behind a hedge of oleanders
and turnsoles cut into arches.]*

LANCÉOR

There is nothing here now but the flowers
of life! . . . Look! . . . They are coming
down, they are streaming down upon us! . . .

They are bursting on the branches, they bend the trees, they entangle our steps, they press against one another, they crush one another, they open out wide, one within the other, they blind the leaves, they dazzle the grass; I know none of them and the spring is drunk; I have never seen flowers so disordered, so resplendent! . . .

JOYZELLE

Where are we? . . .

LANCÉOR

We are in the garden which you would not open to my love . . .

JOYZELLE

What have we done?

LANCÉOR

I have given the kiss that is given but once; and you have spoken the word that is never respoken . . .

JOYZELLE

[*Swooning.*] Lancéor, I am mad, or else we are going to die . . .

38

Joyzelle

LANCÉOR

[*Supporting her.*] Joyzelle, you are turning pale and your dear arms are pressing me as though you feared that a hidden enemy . . .

JOYZELLE

Have you not seen it? . . .

LANCÉOR

What?

JOYZELLE

We are caught in a trap and those flowers are betraying us . . . The birds were silent, the trees were dead, there was nothing here but weeds, which no one dug up . . . I recognize them all and remember their names, which still remind me of their former wretchedness . . . Here is the buttercup, laden with golden disks; the poor pale pimpernel is changed into a bush of lilies; the tall scabious are dropping their petals over our heads; and those purple bells, which shoot up over the wall to tell to the world that they have seen us, are the fox-

glove, which was pining in the shade . . .
It is as though the sky had shed its flowers
. . . Do not look at them; they are here to
ruin us . . . Ah, I am wrong to seek and I
should have understood! . . . He muttered
confused threats . . . Yes, yes, I knew he
had spells at his command . . . They told
me so one day, but I did not believe them
. . . Now it is his time; it is well, it is too
late; but perhaps we shall see that love also
knows . . . [*A horn sounds.*]

LANCÉOR

Hark! . . .

JOYZELLE

It is the horses' hoofs and the horn sound-
ing the recall.   He is returning.   Fly! . . .

LANCÉOR

But you? . . .

JOYZELLE

I have nothing to fear but his hateful
love . . . Go! . . .

Joyzelle

LANCÉOR

. I will stay with you; and, if his violence . . .

JOYZELLE

You will ruin us both . . . Go! . . . Hide there, behind those spurges . . . Whatever he may say, whatever he may do, do not show yourself and fear nothing for me: I shall know how to defend myself . . . Go! . . . He is coming! . . . Go! . . . I hear his voice . . .

> [LANCÉOR *hides behind a cluster of tall spurges. The railed gate opens and* MERLIN *enters the garden.*]

MERLIN

Is he here, Joyzelle? . . .

JOYZELLE

No.

MERLIN

Those flowers do not lie; they inform against love . . . They were your keepers and have been faithful to me . . . I am not cruel and I forgive more than once . . . You can save him by pointing to the bush which hides him . . . [Joy-zelle *stands motionless.*] Do not look at me with those eyes of hatred . . . You will love me one day, for love goes by dark and generous paths . . . Do you not believe that I will keep my promises? . . .

JOYZELLE

No! . . .

MERLIN

I have done nothing, Joyzelle, to deserve such hatred or such an insult . . . Since you wish it, I will let fate take its course . . .

[*A cry of pain is heard from behind the cluster of spurges.*]

JOYZELLE

[*Rushing behind the cluster.*] Lan-céor! . . .

LANCÉOR

Joyzelle! . . . I am hurt . . . An adder has stung me . . .

Joyzelle

It is not an adder . . . It is a horrible animal . . . It is lifting itself against you! . . . Let me crush it underfoot . . . It is foaming . . . It is dead. . . . Lancéor, you are turning pale! . . . Lean on my neck . . . Fear nothing, I am strong . . . Show me your wound . . . Lancéor, I am here . . . Lancéor, answer me! . . .

MERLIN

[*Approaching them and examining the bite.*] The wound is mortal . . . The poison is very slow and its action is strange . . . Do not despair . . . I alone know the remedy . . .

JOYZELLE

Lancéor! Lancéor! Answer me! Answer me! . . .

MERLIN

He will not answer, he is sound asleep . . . Withdraw, Joyzelle, unless you wish this mere sleep to end in the grave . . . Withdraw, Joyzelle: you will not be betraying him; you will be warding off death . . .

43

JOYZELLE

First make the sign that shall restore him
to life!

MERLIN

[*Looking at her gravely.*] I will make the
sign, Joyzelle. [JOYZELLE *exit slowly, turns
back and withdraws at last, before a grave
and imperious gesture from* MERLIN. MER-
LIN, *left alone with* LANCÉOR, *kneels down beside him to dress his wound.*] There, have no
fear, my son, there, it is for your happiness;
and may all my heart open in the first kiss
that I am able to give you. [*He embraces
him long and fervently. Enter* ARIELLE.]

ARIELLE

Master, we must hasten and lay the new
trap.

MERLIN

Will he fall into it?

ARIELLE

Man always falls into a trap, when his instinct leads him; but let us veil his reason,
let us change his character; we shall behold
a sight that will make us smile . . .

MERLIN

I shall not smile, for the sight is a sad one and I do not like to see a noble and beautiful love, a love that believes itself predestined and unparalleled, thus reduced to nothing, at the first proof, in the arms of a phantom . . .

ARIELLE

Lancéor is not free, for he is no longer himself and I have abandoned him to his instinct during the past hour . . .

MERLIN

He ought to have conquered it . . .

ARIELLE

You speak like that because I am submissive: but remember the time when I was less docile.

MERLIN

You think yourself very docile because I have conquered you; but you retain some shadow even in the light in which I have been

able to train you and I find in you a certain
cruelty that takes too great a pleasure in
men's weaknesses . . .

ARIELLE

Men's weaknesses are often necessary to
the purposes of life . . .

MERLIN

What will happen if he yields? . . .

ARIELLE

He will yield: it is written. The question
is if Joyzelle's love will surmount the proof.

MERLIN

And do you not know?

ARIELLE

No; she has a mind which is not wholly
within my sphere, which depends upon a prin-
ciple which I do not know, which I have never
seen except in her and which changes the future . . . I have tried to subdue her; but
she obeys me only in little things. But it is

46

time to act. Go and find Joyzelle and leave
your son to me . . . Go, lest you should
spoil the proof . . . I shall revive him, I
shall renew and make still deeper and blinder
the intoxication into which I have plunged
him; and I shall become visible to his eyes in
order to deceive his kisses . . .

MERLIN

[*In a voice of smiling reproach.*]
Arielle . . .

ARIELLE

Go, let me be . . . You know that kisses
given to poor Arielle pass like the flash of a
wing that closes over running water . . .

[MERLIN *retires to a distance.* ARI-
ELLE *goes towards the marble basin;
and there, half-hidden behind the
hedge of oleanders, she half opens the
veils that cover her, sits on the grassy
steps that surround the basin and
slowly unties her long hair, while*
LANCÉOR *awakes, groping with his
hands.*]

Joyzelle

Where did I fall asleep? Some strange poison has entered my heart . . . I am no longer the same and my mind is wandering . . . I am struggling against the intoxication and I do not know where I am going . . . [*Catches sight of* ARIELLE.] But who is that woman behind the oleanders? [*Approaching the hedge and looking.*] She is beautiful! . . . She is half unclad and her curved foot, like a prudent flower, is trying the water, which smiles and encircles it with pearls . . . She raises her arms to bind her hair; and the light of the sky glides between her shoulders, like gleaming water over marble wings. [*Approaching closer.*] She is beautiful, she is beautiful! . . . I must see her . . . She is turning round and one of her bare breasts, peeping through her tresses, adds rays to the rays that strike it . . . She is listening, she hears; and her wide-open eyes are questioning the roses . . . She has seen me, she hides herself, she is going to fly . . . [*Passing through the hedge.*] No, no, do not fly from me! . . . I have seen you . . . It is too

late! . . . [*Taking* ARIELLE *in his arms.*] I
want to know the name of so pure a vision,
which plunges into darkness all that I have
loved! . . . I want to know also what too
faithful shadow, what profound retreat concealed the marvel which I hold in my
arms! . . . What trees, what caves, what
towers, what walls were able to stifle the
brilliancy of that flesh, the fragrance of that
life, the fire of those eyes? . . . Where were
you hiding, you whom even a blind man
would find without difficulty in a holiday
crowd? . . . No, do not thrust me away:
this is not the passion, the intoxication
of a moment; it is the lasting dizziness of
love! . . . I am at your knees; I humbly
embrace them . . . I give myself to you
alone . . . I am only yours . . . I ask for
nothing but a kiss from your lips to forget
the rest and seal the future . . . Bow down
your head . . . I see it bending towards me,
I see it consenting; and I call for the token
which nothing can efface henceforth . . .
[*He kisses her passionately. A cry of distress is heard from behind the bushes.*] What
is it? . . .

Joyzelle

[ARIELLE *releases herself from his embrace, flies and disappears. Enter* JOYZELLE.]

JOYZELLE

[*Dismayed.*] Lancéor! . . .

LANCÉOR

Why, where do you come from, Joyzelle?

JOYZELLE

I have seen and heard . . .

LANCÉOR

Well, what? . . . What have you seen? . . . Look around you: there is nothing to see . . . The oleanders are in flower, the water in the basin sleeps, the doves are cooing, the water-lilies are opening their petals: that is all that I see, all that you can see . . .

JOYZELLE

Do you love her?

50

Joyzelle

LANCÉOR

Whom? . . .

JOYZELLE

The woman who has just fled.

LANCÉOR

How should I love her? . . . I had never
seen her . . . The woman was there; I happened to pass . . . She gave a loud scream
. . . I ran up . . . She seemed to have lost
her footing and, as I held out my hand to her,
she gave me the kiss which you heard . . .

JOYZELLE

Is it really you speaking? . . .

LANCÉOR

Yes, look at me: it is really and wholly
I . . . Come nearer, touch me if you doubt
it . . .

JOYZELLE

The proof was terrible; but this is
mortal . . .

Joyzelle

LANCÉOR

What? . . .

JOYZELLE

Was this the first time that you saw that woman? . . .

LANCÉOR

Yes.

JOYZELLE

I shall not speak of it again . . . I shall understand, perhaps; in any case, I forgive . . .

LANCÉOR

There is nothing to forgive.

JOYZELLE

What do you say? . . .

LANCÉOR

I say that I have no need for the pardon with which you overwhelm a fault which I have not committed.

JOYZELLE

Which you have not committed? . . .
Then I did not see what I saw nor hear what
I heard? . . .

LANCÉOR

No.

JOYZELLE

Lancéor! . . .

LANCÉOR

Lancéor! Lancéor! . . . If you called me
by my name for a thousand years and more,
it would alter nothing in what was nothing! . . .

JOYZELLE

I do not know what is passing between
your happiness and mine . . . Oh, look
at me and touch my hands, that I may know
where you are! . . . Oh, if you speak like
that, then it was not you whom I saw this
morning in the wonderful garden where I
gave away my soul! . . . No, there is something that is mocking our strength . . .
It is not possible that all is thus lost because
of a single word . . . I am seeking, I am

53

all astray . . . I saw you, then, and saw all
truth and all trust, as one suddenly sees the
sea between the trees! . . . I was sure, I
knew . . . Love did not deceive me . . .
It deceives me now! . . . It cannot be that
all this should crumble away for a yea or a
nay . . . No, no, I will not have it! . . .
Come, it is not too late; we have not yet lost
our happiness . . . It is all in our hands,
which close upon it. . . . What you have
just done was mad, perhaps . . . I forget
it, I laugh at it, I saw nothing, I tell you!
. . . It does not exist: you can wipe it out
with a word . . . You well know, as I do,
that love has words which nothing can resist
and that the greatest fault, when confessed
in a loyal kiss, becomes a truth more beautiful than innocence . . . Speak that word to
me; give me that kiss: confess the truth, confess what I saw, what I heard; and all will
again be pure as it was and I shall recover
all that you gave me . . .

LANCÉOR

I have said what I have said; if you do not
believe me, go away, you annoy me . . .

Joyzelle

Look me in the face . . . Do you love
her, since you lie like that? . . .

LANCÉOR

No, I love no one; and you less than the
others . . .

JOYZELLE

Lancéor! . . . What have I done? . . .
Perhaps, without knowing . . .

LANCÉOR

Nothing; it is not that . . . But I am not
what you thought and I do not care to be
. . . I am like other men; I wish you to know
it and make the best of it . . . I want all
our promises to be scattered to the wind of
some new dream, like this dead leaf which I
crumple in my hand . . . Ah, the love of
women! . . . Well, so much the worse for
them! . . . I shall live like other men in a
faithless world, where no one loves, where all
oaths yield to the first test . . . Ah,
tears! . . . They were bound to come, I expected them! . . . You are hard, I know,

55

and your tears are scarce . . . I count them
drop by drop! . . . You did not love me!
. . . Love which comes thus, at the first call,
is not that on which happiness is based . . .
In any case, it is not that which I hoped
for . . . More tears! . . . They flow too
late! . . . You did not love me, I did not love
you . . . Another would have said . . .
Ah, another would have known! . . . But
you, no, no; go away! . . . Go away, go
away, I say! . . .

[JOYZELLE *moves away silently, sobbing.
When she has taken a few steps, she
turns back, hesitates, looks sadly at*
LANCÉOR *and disappears with a sup-
pressed cry,* "I love you! . . ."
LANCÉOR, *overwhelmed, bewildered,
staggers away and leans against the
trunk of a tree.*]

LANCÉOR

What have I done? . . . I am obeying . . . what? . . . I do not know . . .
What have I said? . . . It is not I speaking . . . I have lost happiness, the present,

the future . . . I am no longer my own
master . . . I do what I hate to do . . . I
do not know who I am . . . Joyzelle! . . .
Ah, my Joyzelle! . . .

[*He falls, sobbing, with his face to the
ground.*]

CURTAIN

ACT III

A Room in the Palace

(Lancéor *is discovered before a mirror. He appears emaciated, bent, aged, unrecognisable.*)

LANCÉOR

WHO am I? In a few hours I have aged thirty years . . . The poison is doing its work and sorrow too . . . I see myself with terror in this mirror which shows me the wreck of myself . . . Yet it does not lie. [*Going to another mirror.*] For here is another that says the same thing . . . unless they all lie, just as everything seems to lie and to mock at me in this extraordinary island. [*He feels his face.*] Alas, they are right! . . . These wrinkles which my hand follows are not formed by

their malevolent crystal . . . They are
in my flesh! . . . And these hideous blem-
ishes which will not come away, I feel them
under my fingers . . . These bent shoulders
refuse to straighten themselves; my hair is
colourless, like pale ashes after the flame
has died away; my eyes, even my eyes hardly
recognise themselves . . . They used to
open, to laugh, to welcome life . . . Now
they blink and their glances avoid me like
the glances of a knave . . . Not a thing
remains to me of what I was; my mother
would pass by me and not see me . . . It is
finished . . . [*Drawing the curtain of a
tall window.*] Let us hide ourselves; let complete dusk cover all this! . . . [*He lies down
in a dark corner of the room.*] I give up, I
consent . . . I have done what love can never
forgive . . . I am losing my life at last, as
I have lost Joyzelle . . . She will not see me
again, I shall not see her again . . .

[*A door opens. Enter* Joyzelle.]

Joyzelle
[*Surprised by the darkness, she stands a*

moment on the threshold. Then, casting her eyes around the room, she perceives LANCÉOR *lying in a corner and rushes towards him with outstretched arms.*] Lancéor! . . . Ah, these last three days I have lived like a mad thing! I looked for you everywhere. I went to the tower. . . . The doors were closed, the windows too. I crouched on the sill to catch a glimpse of your shadow, I called, I screamed, no one answered. . . . But how pale you are, how thin! . . . I am talking to you without thinking. . . . Give me your two hands. . . .

LANCÉOR

You know me? . . .

JOYZELLE

Why not?

LANCÉOR

But then I am not? . . . I am still myself? . . . Look at me! . . . What trace of me remains? . . . [*Going to the window and tearing aside the curtain.*] Look! Look!

. . . What do you know me by? . . . Tell me, is it here? . . . Is it my hands, my eyes, my clothes, perhaps? . . .

JOYZELLE

[*Looking at him and throwing herself, weeping, in his arms.*] Oh, how you have suffered! . . .

LANCÉOR

I have suffered, yes, I have suffered! . . . I deserved it but too well, after what I said, after what I did! . . . But that is not what matters or overwhelms me . . . I would willingly die, if you could but see once more, were it only for the flash of an eye, that which you once loved . . . I cling to myself, to the little that remains of me . . . I should like to hide myself, to bury my distress; and yet I want you to see me first, so that you may know at last what you would have to love, if you still loved me . . . Come, come, nearer, nearer . . . Not nearer to me, but nearer to the rays that shine upon my wretchedness . . . Look at these wrinkles, these dead eyes, these lips

Joyzelle

. . . No, no, do not approach, lest disgust . . . I am less like myself than if I had returned from a world which life had never visited . . . You do not recoil? You are not astonished? . . . You do not see me as these mirrors see me? . . .

JOYZELLE

I see that you are pale and that you seem tired . . . Do not put away my arms . . . Bring your face closer . . . Why not let me put my lips to it, as I did when all things smiled to us in the garden of flowers? . . . Love knows many days when nothing smiles . . . . What matter, if it be there to smile when we weep? . . . I am pushing back your hair which hid your face and made it look so sad . . . See, it is just like that which I pushed back in our first kiss . . . Come, come, do not think about the lies of the mirrors . . . They do not know what they say; but love knows . . . Already life is returning to those eyes which see me again . . . Have no fear, for I have none . . . I know what we must do and I shall have the secret that will cure your pain . . .

62

Joyzelle

LANCÉOR

Joyzelle! . . .

JOYZELLE

Yes, yes, come nearer; I love you more dearly than at the happy moment when all united us . . .

LANCÉOR

Ah, I understand that; but the other, the other thing! . . .

JOYZELLE

What thing?

LANCÉOR

I understand that one can find one's love in ruins, that one can gather up its remnants and love them still . . . But where are the remnants of our love? Nothing is left of it; for, before fate struck me as you see, I had crushed out of existence all that it could not destroy . . . I have lied and deceived; and, at the very moment when the least lie begins again in a sphere where nothing is wiped

out, a fault which love might have pardoned
. . . Truth is dead in our one heart . . . I
have lost the confidence in which all my
thoughts surrounded your thoughts, even as a
transparent water surrounds a still clearer
water . . . I myself no longer believe in it, I
no longer believe in myself; I have nothing
pure left into which you can bend to find my
shadow; and my soul is even sadder than my
body . . .

JOYZELLE

Did you kiss that woman? . . .

LANCÉOR

Yes.

JOYZELLE

Did she call you? . . .

LANCÉOR

No.

JOYZELLE

And why did you say that I was mistaken? . . .

Joyzelle

LANCÉOR

What good would it be to tell you, Joyzelle? It is too late . . . You would not
believe me, for you would have to believe the
incredible . . . I was walking in a trance,
in a sort of invincible, mocking dream . . .
My mind, my reason, my will were all further
from themselves than is this shattered body
from what it was . . . I would have liked to
tell you, to shout to you again and again that
I was a lie that had escaped control and that
the shameful speeches that defiled my lips
stifled, in spite of myself, the tearful con-
fession and the ardent words of desperate
love that were leaping towards you . . . I
made efforts fit to burst my throat, to break
my heart; and I heard my faithless voice
betray me; and my arms, my hands, my eyes,
my kisses were powerless to disown it; for,
except my soul, which you did not see, I felt
myself a prey to a hostile force, irresistible,
alas, and incomprehensible! . . .

JOYZELLE

But ah, I did see it! . . . And I knew at

once that it was not you that were lying;
that it was impossible . . .

LANCÉOR

How did you know? . . .

JOYZELLE

Because I love you. . . .

LANCÉOR

But what am I, Joyzelle, what do you love
in me, in whom I have profaned and others
destroyed all that you once loved? . . .

JOYZELLE

You.

LANCÉOR

What remains of me? . . . Not these
hands, which have lost their strength; not
these eyes, which no longer have their bright-
ness; not this heart, which has betrayed
love . . .

JOYZELLE

It is you and still you and none but you
yourself! . . . What matter who you are, so

66

long as I find you! . . . Oh, I cannot tell how to explain that! . . . When one loves as I love you, she is blind and deaf, because she looks beyond and listens elsewhere . . . When she loves as I love you, it is not what he says, it is not what he does, it is not what he is that she loves in the man she loves: it is he and only he, who remains the same, through the passing years and troubles . . . It is he alone, it is you alone, in whom no change can come but that which increases love . . . He who is all in you, you who are all in him, whom I see, whom I hear, to whom I listen incessantly and whom I love always . . .

LANCÉOR

Joyzelle! . . .

JOYZELLE

Yes, yes, embrace me, crush me in your arms! . . . We have to struggle, we shall have to suffer; we are here in a world that seems full of snares . . . We are only two, but we are all love! . . .

Joyzelle

(*A grove.* JOYZELLE *lies sleeping on a grassy bank, before a box hedge, cut into arches, in which lilies are flowering. It is night. A fountain ripples gently. The moon is shining.*)

[*Enter* ARIELLE.]

ARIELLE

She sleeps . . . The breaths of the garden are hushed around her to listen to her breath; and the nightingale alone, deputed by the night which bathes her in silver, comes to soothe her slumbers . . . How beautiful and peaceful she is; and how pure she looks, a thousand times purer than the water that trickles yonder, flowing from the glaciers, in the snowy whiteness that sings under the pale leaves! . . . Her sweet hair lies spread like a flood of motionless light; and the moon cannot tell to whom belongs the gold that mingles with the azure in which its beams float . . . Her bright eyes are closed; and yet the light

that falls from the stars tremulously raises
her loving eyelids to seek beneath them the
last memory of the fair day that is past
. . . Her mouth is a moist, breathing flower;
and the lilies have poured dew-drops on her
bare shoulder, to give her her share of the
pearls which night distributes in silence, in
the name of the heavens that open over the
treasure of the worlds . . . Ah, Joyzelle,
Joyzelle! I am but a phantom lost in the
night, more lost than you, for all my clear-
sightedness, and nearer the tomb where happiness expires . . . I am not my own mis-
tress; I obey my master, I can give nothing
but an invisible kiss, which cannot wake you
and is not even mine . . . But I love you,
I love you, as a less happy sister loves her
whom love has chosen first . . . I love
you, I encompass you with all the powers
that are not named in the prayers of men;
and I would that my master had met you
earlier, before fate, which hurries forward
that incomparable hour, had fixed the tearful
future that awaits him and awaits me with
him . . . I spread my powerless, troubled
affection over your calm sleep . . . Here is

the only kiss that I can give you . . . Ah,
why does not he of whom I am but the uncon-
scious and docile shadow come himself to lay
it on your lips, which call to mine even as all
that is beautiful calls to mystery! . . . [*She
kisses* JOYZELLE *on the forehead.*]

JOYZELLE

[*In her sleep.*] Lancéor! . . .

ARIELLE

One more . . . The last, even as we drink
of the well defended by the angels who keep
the secrets of time and space, the well at
whose brink we shall never rest again . . .

JOYZELLE

[*Sleeping, talking as in a dream.*] Is that
you, Lancéor? . . . How sweet your lips are
at the breath of dawn! . . . I sink beneath
the flowers that fall from paradise . . .

ARIELLE

Faithful in sleep and constant in her
dreams! . . . The demons of the night will
steal nothing from the love that fills the past

and future of a heart! . . . Ah, my master
and father! . . . It is she whom your only
hope awaited, in vain, to avert the fate that
threatens your old age! . . . O master, if
you be willing, there is yet time; and happiness is here: you have but to gather it! . . .
It sways uncertain between your son and you;
a gesture would be enough to fix it upon ourselves . . . Come hither, she is yours! . . .
Come, come, come, I am calling you . . . I
know that I am right and that man must not
renounce life and ruin himself to save those
whom he loves . . .

MERLIN

[*In the distance, in a voice of grave reproach.*] Arielle! . . .

[*He enters, wrapped in a long cloak.*]

ARIELLE

I am speaking for you and my voice is
your voice . . . I speak in the name of your
heart, which loves deeply and dares not confess it . . . You had, at this prescribed
moment, to meet that sleeping woman, in

71

order to avoid one who will destroy your old
age . . .

MERLIN

Begone, it is too late . . .

ARIELLE

No, it is not too late; this is the one moment; and your destiny depends on the movement which you make . . .

MERLIN

Begone, do not tempt me, or I will plunge
you back into your impotent shade . . . I
drew you from it to open my eyes and not to
mislead me . . .

ARIELLE

To listen to the instinct by which alone
men are saved is not to be misled . . . Think
of the terrible days which Viviane is preparing: Viviane, whom you must love if you do
not love this one . . .

MERLIN

Viviane? . . . Is it in this life or in some
other world that that name resounds within

my secret heart like a name of madness, sorrow and shame? . . .

ARIELLE

No, it is in this life, the only one that you possess . . . It is the name of the fairy who, in Brocéliande, where your fate leads you, awaits your coming to shatter your old age . . . O master, I see her! . . . Have a care, she approaches and will win your heart! . . . So soon as this love, so pure, so healthful, shall have lost its claims, hers crawls out of the shadow . . . Master, I entreat you! . . . My eyes are counting her wiles: she entwines you with her arms which travesty love; she takes away your power, your reason, your wisdom; she snatches from you at last the secret of your strength; and, like an old, drunken man, you fall to the ground . . . Then she strips you, mocks at you, stands erect again and closes on us the door of the mortal cavern which will never open again . . .

MERLIN

It is inevitable, then? . . .

73

Joyzelle

ARIELLE

You know as I do, that nothing can deceive
me where you are concerned . . . Master, I
beseech you, both for yourself and for me,
who love the light and who must lose it with
you! . . . This is the irrevocable hour! . . .
Choose, choose life! . . . It still offers itself
and therefore it belongs to us, and you have
a right to it! . . .

MERLIN

Begone, it is useless . . . Besides, this one
would never have loved me . . .

ARIELLE

It is enough that you love her and that he
whom she loves no longer stands between you
. . . That is what I read in the two fu-
tures . . .

MERLIN

[*Wiping the sweat of anguish from his
brow.*] Begone, for I know . . . And so it
was written that, by loving this child, I could
have saved myself . . . But she is not for
me; and my hour is past . . . This is the

74

hour of those who come and who have met as
time ordained, as life ordained . . . Begone,
begone, I say! . . .

[ARIELLE, *veiling her features, exit
silently.*]

I surrender my share; and it is for you, my
son, that I complete the proof . . . [*He
takes off his cloak and appears taller and
younger, dressed in clothes similar to* LANCÉ-
OR'S *and presenting a strange resemblance
to him. Approaching* JOYZELLE.] Ah, my
innocent Joyzelle! . . . You will suffer too,
you must suffer still more, since destiny lies
hidden in your tears; but what matter
the sorrows that lead to love? . . . I would
gladly exchange all the joys that I have
known in my poor life for the most
cruel of those happy sorrows . . . [*He leans
over* JOYZELLE.] Arielle spoke truly. I
have but to make a movement to put back the
hours and the days and thus escape the horrible end which fate reserves for me . . . Yes,
but that movement destroys him whom I love
more than myself, him whom the years have

chosen for the love for which I had hoped
. . . Ah, when we thus hold in our hands our
own happiness and that of another man ; when
we must crush one so that the other may sur-
vive: it is then that we feel how deep are the
roots that bind us to the earth on which we
suffer; it is then that life utters a superhuman
cry to make itself heard and to defend its
rights ! . . . But it is then also that we must
give ear to the other voice that speaks, to
the voice that has nothing definite or sure to
tell us, that has nothing to promise and
that is only a murmur more sacred than
life's inarticulate cries . . . Lancéor and
Joyzelle, love each other, love me, for I have
loved you . . . I am weak and frail and
made for happiness like other men ; nor do
I surrender my share without a struggle
. . . Love each other, my children ; I am
listening to the little voice which has nothing
to tell me, but which alone is right . . . [*He
kneels before* JOYZELLE *and kisses her on the
forehead.*]

JOYZELLE
[*Waking with a start.*] Lancéor ! . . .

76

Joyzelle

MERLIN

Yes, it is I: the darkness has led me to you;
and I come to wake you with a new kiss, so
that you may . . .

JOYZELLE

[*Springing up and looking at him in terror.*] Who are you? . . .

MERLIN

[*Putting out his arms to embrace her.*]
You know who I am, Joyzelle, and love must
tell you . . .

JOYZELLE

[*Drawing back violently.*] Ah, do not
touch me, or I shall summon death to come
to put an end to this horrible dream! . . .
I know not what phantoms have haunted this
night, but this is the vilest, the basest, the
most cowardly that the darkness has sent!
. . . I do not believe in it yet! . . . I am
bruising my eyes in trying to awake myself! . . . Ah, do not come near me! . . .

Joyzelle

Back! . . . Begone! . . . You fill me with horror! . . .

MERLIN

Look at me, Joyzelle! . . . I do not understand you; and doubtless sleep still troubles . . .

JOYZELLE

Where is he? . . .

MERLIN

Wake, Joyzelle . . .

JOYZELLE

Where is he and what have you done with him? . . .

MERLIN

He is wherever I am; and, if your eyes mislead you . . .

JOYZELLE

Do you not know that I carry him here, in these eyes which see you and compare what he is with what you are? . . . Have you not seen what he is in my heart, that you should

78

copy him thus? . . . You, beside him; you,
in his clothes and under his aspect: ah, it is
as though death pretended to be life! . . .
But there might be twenty thousand of you
resembling him and he alone be changed from
what he was yesterday; and I would sweep
away the twenty thousand phantoms, to go
to the only man who is not a dream among
the other dreams! . . . Oh, do not try to hide
in the shadow . . . You retreat too late; I
have discovered you and I know who you are
. . . I know your spells; and how I should
laugh at them, did I not fear that, by your
witchcraft, when usurping that dear and unrecognisable shape, you have caused him to
suffer! . . . What have you done to him?
. . . Where is he? . . . I will know . . .
You shall not go without answering . . .
[*Seizing* MERLIN's *hand.*] I am alone, I am
weak . . . But I insist, I insist . . . I will
know, I will know! . . .

MERLIN

I love you too much, Joyzelle, to do him
any harm, so long as you love him . . . He

has therefore nothing to fear . . . Do you
not fear me either. I am not here to take advantage of the darkness and surprise your
heart. I had another object . . . Listen to
me, Joyzelle; it is no longer the rival or the
unhappy lover that speaks to you; it is a
prudent and anxious father . . . Before he
came who conquered you, as never man in this
world conquered woman, I had, I confess,
caught a glimpse of a happiness which it is
idle to pursue in the decline of years . . .
To-day I retire, sadly, but in good faith . . .
I know how much you love the poor uncon-
scious being whom malevolent chance has
placed upon your road . . . And do not
mistake me; I am speaking of him now without hatred or envy, but not without dismay,
when I think of the heart-rending days which
he is preparing for you . . . That is why I
insist on enlightening you as regards him, at
the risk of displeasing you . . . I have no
other care than to make you turn away from
an unhappy love in which nothing but tears
and disillusion await you . . . I have no
hope for myself . . . I do not ask you to
love me in his stead . . . You have shown me

Joyzelle

fully that that is impossible . . . I desire
only that you will cease to love him: that is
all that I implore of the kindness of fate;
and fate to-night hears my prayer . . .

JOYZELLE

How? . . .

MERLIN

The proof is grave and sad; I would have
liked to spare you . . . But you know better
than I that there are salutary sufferings,
before which it is shameful to fly . . . A
sign will be enough to overturn a world
. . . A little movement of that neck which
as yet bends without anxiety, a single glance
of those eyes, too confident and too full of innocence, will destroy before my sight the most
beautiful thing that love has created in a
woman's heart . . . And yet, it must be
. . . It is right, it is well that this thing
should to-day be lost in tears which it may
yet be possible to wipe away; for later it
would have had to sink in sorrows which
nothing could have consoled . . .

Joyzelle

What do you mean? . . .

MERLIN

That, at this very moment, when all that is spotless and true, limpid and ardent in your heart, when all the transparent virtues of your soul, all the faithfulness, all the loyalty and all the innocence of your virgin blood mount up towards him whom you had selected to make of him the purest, the happiest of men, he is there, behind us, at two steps from this bank, sheltered by those leaves which he thinks impenetrable, in the arms of the woman with whom, the other day, as you yourself saw, he profaned the marvellous love which you have given him! . . .

JOYZELLE

No.

MERLIN

Why do you say no, without looking? . . .

JOYZELLE

Because he is myself . . .

82

MERLIN

I do not ask you to believe my words: I simply ask you to turn your head . . .

JOYZELLE

No.

MERLIN

Do you hear the murmur of their voices mingling and the song of kisses answering kisses? . . .

JOYZELLE

No.

MERLIN

Do not raise your voice to interrupt a crime which you do not wish to see . . . They will not hear you; they listen only to the sound of their lips! . . . But turn, Joyzelle, I beseech you! . . . Your life is at stake and all the happiness to which you have a right! . . . Do not reject the proffered truth that comes to save you if you have the courage at last to accept it! It will not return except to make you weep, when it is

83

too late! . . . But look! Look! . . . You
need not even turn your head! . . . Your
star is kind to you and does not tire! . . .
Do not close your eyes, it is coming to un-
seal them! . . . See! . . . The shadow of
their arms, lengthened by the moonlight, is
creeping through that arch and covering
your knees! . . . Open your eyes! Look!
. . . It is coming to defy you, it is rising to
your lips! . . .

JOYZELLE

No.

[*A pause.*]

MERLIN

I understand you, Joyzelle . . . You must
not deny what remains of your love while I
am here . . . I leave you to yourself, face
to face with your duty, face to face with your
destiny . . . Such sacrifices ask for no wit-
nesses: they demand silence . . . The truth
is there; it is cowardly to fly from it . . .
You will know how to face it when you are
alone . . . There is yet time . . . I admire you, Joyzelle. . . . Your life and your

happiness invoke your courage and depend
upon a glance . . .

> [*Exit* MERLIN. JOYZELLE, *for a long
> moment, remains seated on the bank,
> motionless, with wide-open eyes,
> staring fixedly before her. Then
> she rises, draws herself up and goes
> out slowly, without turning her
> head.*]

CURTAIN

ACT IV

A Room in the Palace

(*At the back, to the right, is a large marble
bed, on which* LANCÉOR *is lying lifeless.*
JOYZELLE, *anxious, dishevelled, is busy-
ing herself around him.*)

JOYZELLE

Lancéor! Lancéor! . . . He cannot hear
me . . . His eyes are wide open . . .
Lancéor, I am here, I am bending over your
eyes . . . Look at me, look at me! . . . No,
he does not see me! . . . Lancéor, for pity's
sake! . . . If your voice is too weak, give a
sign of life! . . . I take you in my arms, my
arms that love you! . . . Come, come, come
to yourself, in our great love! . . . See, see,
it is my hands that are lifting your head
. . . Do you recognise my hands, as they
stroke your hair? . . . You so often told
me, when we were happy, that the least
86

caress of these dear hands would recall
your soul, even from the greatest happiness
of paradise, from the greatest darkness of
. . . No, no, it is not there! . . . But his
head is drooping, his arm falls back lifeless
and his fingers seem to me colder than this
marble . . . [*Mechanically feeling one of the
columns of the bed.*] No, it is not that
. . . But I must know . . . And his eyes
are no longer . . . [*Raising his head.*] Is
it his or mine that are so dim? . . . No, it is
impossible! . . . No, no, I will not have it!
Ah, I will open your lips! . . . [*She places
her lips on* LANCÉOR's.] Lancéor! Lancéor!
All the ardour of my life shall enter
your heart! . . . Do not fear, do not fear!
It is the saving flame and life that restores life! . . . Breathe it all in the last
efforts of my breath which loves you! . . . I
would gladly suffocate in exchanging my life
for yours! . . . I give you my strength, my
hours, my years! . . . Here they are, here
they are! . . . You have but to make a
movement, to open your lips! . . . It must
be so! . . . It must be possible thus to give
new life to those whom we love better than

ourselves! . . . When we give them all, they cannot but take it! . . . [*Raising her head to look at* LANCÉOR.] He is falling back! He is going from me! . . . [*Infatuated, she takes him in her arms again.*] Help! . . . No, this is too much! . . . Help! Hasten! Hasten! . . . Ah no, I know better, no, no, it is not that . . . Death does not come like this when love threatens it! . . . No, no, I fear nothing, no, no, I will not have it! . . . But I am crying for help! I cannot remain alone, I cannot fight alone against all the strength of death approaching! . . . If no one comes, it will end by conquering! . . . Help, I say! . . . You must come to my aid! . . . Life must help me, or it is no longer possible and we shall succumb! . . . [*She falls sobbing on* LANCÉOR's *lifeless body.*]

[*Enter* MERLIN.]

MERLIN

I am here, Joyzelle . . .

JOYZELLE

[*Starting up, as though to go to him,*

while still holding LANCÉOR *in a close embrace.*] Ah, it is you! . . . So it is you! . . . At last there is help and life coming! . . . Look at him! See! . . . It is time, he is falling back! . . . I fling myself at your feet! . . . Yes, yes, you can do all; and I have seen clear in all things! . . . Ah, at such moments as this, one would see clear in the depths of a darkness which worlds have never traversed! . . . Oh, I entreat you, tell me what to do! . . . I am no longer Joyzelle, I am no longer fierce and I have no more pride . . . I am broken and dead: I drag myself at your feet; and it is no more a question of this or that, of love or kisses, or of trifling things! . . . Life and death stand face to face, they are fighting under our eyes and must be separated . . . You do not move a step! . . . Ah, I know how great your hatred is and how you detest that defenceless man . . . Yes, you are right, he is anything you please, he is a coward, he is a rascal, he is your enemy, he is a twenty-fold traitor, since you will have it so! . . . Yes, I admit it, I was wrong, I confess it, and I no longer love him, since you wish it, and I

am ready for anything, provided he be saved!
. . . But that must be done and that counts
and all the rest is madness! . . . But come,
come, come, I tell you death is triumphing
and will carry him off! . . . See, his hands
are turning blue and his eyes are growing
dull and it is horrible! . . .

MERLIN

Joyzelle, fear nothing; his life is in my
hands and I will save him, if you wish me to
save him . . .

JOYZELLE

If I wish you to save him! . . . But do
you not see that, if you were to hesitate, do
you not know that, if for his sake, I had to
. . . No, no, I meant to say . . . my distress
bewilders me . . . He has ceased to breathe,
I no longer hear his heart . . . You seem to
me so slow! . . . Do you think that there is
no danger, no need for haste? . . . I will
speak no more; I am making you lose minutes
which perhaps were passing to save him . . .
If you will not help him yourself—and I can
understand that, for you do not love him—

tell me only what I must do to assist him; and I shall know how to do it . . . But I can see, I am sure that he cannot wait and that we must make haste . . .

MERLIN

I have told you, Joyzelle, his life is in my hands and cannot escape without my consent. I warned you of it. The poison is doing its work and I can see it. I alone can cure him, snatch him from death, call back his vigour, his beauty, which are fading away, and restore him to you as he was before . . .

JOYZELLE

Ah, I entreat you, do not dally thus! . . . What is his beauty to me, if his life escapes us! . . . Give him back to me as he is, whatever he may be; what care I, if only I have him back, if only he breathes! . . .

MERLIN

Yes, I will give him back to you. I have already twice done—and each time repented —what I will do again for the last time, since you ask it: but it is a sacrifice which none but you could have obtained. By restoring his life, I risk my own. To rouse his strength, to recall his soul, I must give him a part of my strength, a part of my soul. It may be that he will take from me more than I have left and that I shall fall dead beside the rival whom I shall have restored to life . . . Time was when I would thus risk my existence to save a stranger by the wayside, almost without hesitating and without asking anything in exchange . . . But to-day I am more prudent and more wise. As I am offering my life, it is but fair that I should be paid for it and paid in advance; and I will give it to him only if you promise me the dearest moment of your own . . .

JOYZELLE

How? . . . What am I to do? . . .

MERLIN

[*Aside.*] O poor and all too innocent child! . . . And you, my chaste thoughts, oh, take no part in the odious words which my voice must now spread around their love! . . . I blush at the proof and am ashamed of what I

am now compelled to say . . . You will forgive me when you know all . . . It is not
I that speak: it is the future, which man
ought not to know, the shameless, pitiless future, which reveals a day and throws light
upon a destiny only to conceal the rest and
which wishes that I should know whether you
are she whom it marks out . . .

JOYZELLE

What are you saying? . . . Why do you
hesitate? . . . There is nothing in the world;
examine myself as I may, I see nothing in the
world, in our world or in the other, that I
could be asked and not be ready to . . .

MERLIN

See: I will cease talking in riddles . . .
That man whom you see and whom you hold
pressed in your arms lies stretched as near
death as though he were laid on the slab
of his tomb . . . A movement can bring him
back to life; a movement can make him fall
on the other side . . . Well, at the very moment when you say yes and before the echo
which slumbers yonder under those marble

93

vaults has time to repeat that you have consented, I will make the certain movement which will snatch him from the darkness, provided that you promise to come to-night, here, in this room in which I shall restore him to you and on this same bed over which you are leaning, to give yourself to me, without shame, without reserve . . .

JOYZELLE

I? . . . Give myself to you? . . .

MERLIN

Yes.

JOYZELLE

I, give myself to you, when he is restored to me? . . .

MERLIN

So that he may be restored to you.

JOYZELLE

No, I have not understood . . . There are words, no doubt, which I do not understand . . . No, it is not possible that a man who is not one of the princes of hell should come thus, at the moment when all love's sorrow

knows not what to hope for or what to undertake . . . No, I have mistaken you and
am doing you an injury . . . You must
forgive me; I am a virgin, I am ignorant,
I do not quite know what those words imply
. . . But I see now . . . Yes, you are right
. . . Yes, yes, you mean to say that it is
fair that I should bear a share of the danger
and that my life should be joined for a moment to yours, in order to create the other life
which is to revive him . . . But I want that
share, I want it for myself alone, I want the
whole of it, the greatest possible share, and
I never hoped that it could be given me! . . .

MERLIN

Joyzelle, time presses . . . Do not seek
elsewhere: you know what I am asking and
the word means all that you dare not believe . . .

JOYZELLE

Then, at the very moment when he comes
back to me, when I see him once more breathing in my arms and smiling at the love which
he will have found again, I shall have to

snatch from him all that I have given? . . .
But what remains for him if you take everything from us; and what shall I tell him when
he kisses me? . . .

MERLIN

You will tell him nothing, if you wish for
his happiness . . .

JOYZELLE

But I must tell him everything, since I
love him! . . . No, no, I can see clearly, that
cannot be, that does not exist; and there must
be gods or demons to prevent such things: if
not, I cannot see why one should wish to live
. . . I have confidence in them, I have confidence in you . . . It was only a proof; and
all this is not, cannot be real . . . It seems
to me that already you look at me with less
ill-will . . . See, I beseech you, I throw
myself at your feet and kiss your hands
. . . I will confess all to you . . . I did
not love you, you hated him too much; but I
never believed that you were unjust or unworthy of love . . . When you came in, I
did not hesitate, I went up to you, I asked

you to snatch from death the only man I
love; and yet I knew that you loved me too
. . . But, I do not know why, my instinct
told me that you were generous and capable
of doing what I would have done for you,
what he himself would have done; and, when
you have done what we would have done, you
shall have in our hearts a part of our love
that is not the least good part, nor the
least fine, nor the most perishable . . .

MERLIN

Yes, I know: when I have given him back
his life, at the risk of my own, he will have
the kisses, the lips and the eyes, the days
and nights, all, in short, that forms love's
vain and ephemeral happiness! . . . But I,
I shall have something much better; and sometimes, by chance, in passing, I shall be
vouchsafed a kindly smile, which will not
perish, provided that I refrain from demand-
ing it too often . . . No, Joyzelle, at my
age we are no longer satisfied with illusions
of that kind nor with those deceptive dregs.
The hour of heroic falsehoods is past for me.
I wish to have what he will have. I care little

for your smile, which I know to be impossible:
I want yourself; I want you absolutely, were
it only for a moment; but I shall have that
moment: he will give it me . . . [*Approaching* LANCÉOR.] Look at him, Joyzelle: his features are becoming distorted; we
have waited too long and the danger increases with each minute that passes . . .
Will you come? . . .

JOYZELLE

[*Casting a bewildered glance around her.*]
Nothing bursts, nothing falls and I am
alone in the world! . . .

MERLIN

[*Feeling* LANCÉOR's *body.*] The danger is
becoming grave. . . . I know the symptoms . . .

JOYZELLE

Well, then, yes, I will come! . . . I will
come to-night! I will come this evening! . . .
But save him first and restore him to life!
. . . See, his eyes are hollowing and his
lips are fading and I stand here bargain-

ing for his life, as though it were a question of . . .

MERLIN

He shall be restored to you; but remember, Joyzelle, if you are not true to your promise, the hand that cures him will strike him mercilessly . . .

JOYZELLE

But I shall be true to it and I would go on my knees to the end of the other world to remain true to it! . . . Ah, I will come, I tell you! I give myself absolutely and I am wholly yours! . . . What more do you want? . . . I have nothing left! . . .

MERLIN

It is well; I have your promise; I will fulfill mine. . . . [*Aside, taking* LANCÉOR *in his arms.*] Forgive me, my son, in the name of your destiny, which demands this torture . . . [*He leans over* LANCEOR *and presses a long kiss on his eyelids and lips. Aloud.*] See, he returns from the regions without light . . . Life is restored to him, but he

99

will awake only in your eager arms. I leave
you to your work. Remember your word . . .

[*Exit* MERLIN. JOYZELLE *has taken*
LANCÉOR *in her arms and looks at
him in anguish. Soon her lover's
eyes half open and his hands move
feebly.*]

JOYZELLE

Lancéor! . . . His eyes have opened and
closed again and I saw the light bathe in
their blue! And here are his hands, which
seem to seek mine! . . . Here they are,
Lancéor, here they are in your own, which
are no longer frozen! . . . They dare not
leave them, lest they should lose them; and
yet I would support your shoulder and embrace your neck which droops upon my
breast . . . Ah, all the good things are returning and returning together! . . . I hear
his heart beat, I breathe his breath: they
took all away from me, but they have given
it all back! . . . Listen to me, Lancéor: I
want to see you, I am looking for your
face, do not hide your forehead in my hair,

which loves you; my eyes love you still more and want their share too! . . . [LAN-CÉOR *lifts his head a little.*] Oh, he has heard me and listened to me! . . . He is here, he is here, there is no doubt of it now, he is here, before me, more living than life! . . . He is here before me; and the roses of dawn and the flowers of awakening have brought colour to his cheeks and are covering his smile, for he smiles already as though he saw me! . . . Ah, the gods are too good! . . . They have pity on men! . . . There are skies that open! There are gods of love! There are gods of life! . . . We must thank them and love one another, since they also love! . . . Come, come, come to my arms; your eyes still seek me, but your lips find me . . . They open at last to call to mine; and mine are here, carrying all love! . . .

> [*A pause; she kisses him long and eagerly.*]

LANCÉOR

[*Recovering consciousness.*] Joyzelle. . . .

JOYZELLE

Yes, yes, it is I, it is I; look at me,

look! . . . Here are my hands, my forehead,
my hair, my shoulder. . . . And here are my
kisses, which yours recognise! . . .

LANCÉOR

Yes, it is you, it is indeed you, it is you
and the light . . . And then this room, too,
which I saw before. . . . Wait a little . . .
What happened to me? . . . I remember, I
remember . . . I was lying yonder, yonder,
I know not where, before great doors which
some one was trying to open . . . I was
buried and was turning cold . . . And then
I called to you, I called without ceasing and
you did not come . . .

JOYZELLE

But I did, I came, I was there, I was
there! . . .

LANCÉOR

No, you were not there . . . I was seized
with icy coldness, I was seized with darkness
and I was losing my life . . . But now it is
you! . . . Yes, yes, my eyes see you, they
behold you suddenly as they emerge from the

dark . . . Scared though they be by the glaring light, it is you they see and I am passing from the tomb to the joy of the sunlight in the arms of love! That seems impossible to one coming from so far! . . . I must touch you, I must cling to the caresses of your hands, to the light of your eyes, I must seize the real gold of the hair that bears witness to the daylight! . . . Oh, you could never believe how one loves when dying, nor how I mean to love you after losing you and finding you again! . . .

JOYZELLE
I too; I too! . . .

LANCÉOR
And the joy of returning to the arms which press you and which still tremble, because they had ceased to hope! . . . Do you feel yours quiver and mine adore you? . . . They seek, they enlace one another, they fear lest they should lose one another, they no longer dare to open . . . They no longer obey, they do not know that they are hurting us and are like to stifle us in their blind intoxi-

cation! . . . Ah, they know at last the worth
of clasping a glowing body; and one would
die to learn life and to know love! . . .

JOYZELLE

Yes, one would die . . .

LANCÉOR

It is strange: when I was down there, in
the frozen region, some one approached whom
I thought I recognised . . .

JOYZELLE

It was he.

LANCÉOR

Who?

JOYZELLE

The lord of the island.

LANCÉOR

He? . . . But he hated me . . .

JOYZELLE

It was he.

LANCÉOR

I do not quite understand . . . Did he

then bring me back to love, to life? . . . Was he willing to restore me to her who loved me and whom he loved himself? . . .

JOYZELLE

Yes.

LANCÉOR

But why did he do it? . . .

JOYZELLE

I besought him until he consented.

LANCÉOR

Did he hesitate?

JOYZELLE

Yes.

LANCÉOR

Why?

JOYZELLE

He said that, in saving your life, he risked his own.

LANCÉOR

Nothing compelled him to it . . . And then, quite simply, he gave back life to the only man who is taking away all hope of the

love that would make the happiness of his
life? . . .

JOYZELLE

Yes.

LANCÉOR

And without asking anything, from kindness, from pity, from generosity? . . .

JOYZELLE

Yes.

LANCÉOR

Ah, we were unjust and our worst enemies
are better than we believe! . . . There are
treasures of nobility and love even in the
heart of hatred! . . . And this thing which
he has done! . . . No, I really do not know
that I could have done as much; and I would
never have thought that that poor old man
. . . But is it not almost incredible, Joyzelle, and is it not heroic? . . .

JOYZELLE

Yes.

LANCÉOR

Where is he? We must go and fling ourselves at his feet, confess our error, wipe out the injustice of which we were guilty when we did not love him . . . He must have his part and the best part of the happiness which he restores to us! . . . He must have our hearts, our joy, our smile and our tears of love, all that one can give to those who give all! . . .

JOYZELLE

We will go, we will go . . .

LANCÉOR

Joyzelle, what is it? . . . You scarcely answer me . . . I do not know if my senses are still in the power of the night whence I am issuing, but I do not recognise your words and your movements . . . You seem to be seeking, doubting, dreaming . . . And I, who return to you full of love and joy, find so little of either in your eyes, which avoid me, in your hands, which forget me . . . What has happened? . . . Why recall me and restore me to life, if, during my absence, I have lost what I love? . . .

Joyzelle

JOYZELLE

Oh no, no, Lancéor, you have not lost me! . . .

LANCÉOR

Your voice seeks a smile and finds but a sob . . .

JOYZELLE

Yes, I wanted to smile and I am smiling now . . . But do not be surprised: I have wept so long and so desperately that the tears still rise in spite of myself . . . Joy was so far away that it could not return with the first kisses . . . It will need many before it recovers confidence in my heart; and I am almost sad in the midst of my happiness . . .

LANCÉOR

Oh, my poor Joyzelle! . . . Is that what your grave silence means? . . . And I was distressing myself like a stupid child! . . . I am thinking only of myself, I am drunk with life and understand nothing . . . I was forgetting that in your place I should have lost courage . . . It is true, you are right, it is you, not I, returning from death; and, when two beings love as we do, the one that does not die is the only one that really dies . . . Do not hide your tears . . . The sadder you appear, the more I feel that you love me . . . Now it is for me to take care of you, now it is for me to call back your soul, to warm your disconcerted hands, to pursue your lips and bring you back to the midst of the happiness which we had lost . . . We shall soon be there, since love is our guide . . . It triumphs over everything when it finds two hearts that give themselves to it fearlessly and without reserve . . . All the rest is nothing, all the rest is forgotten, all the rest withdraws to make way for love . . .

JOYZELLE

[*Staring fixedly before her.*] All the rest withdraws to make way for love . . .

CURTAIN

ACT V

SCENE I

A Gallery in the Palace

[*Enter* MERLIN *and* LANCÉOR.]

FATHER! . . . Then it is true and you are my father! . . . And indeed it seems to me, since you told me, as though I had always known it in my far-seeing heart . . . [*Coming closer.*] But how wonderful it is! . . . I see you again at last as I saw you amid my childish sports; and, when I look at you, I see myself in a graver, nobler and more powerful mirror than those which reflect my features along this room. But what will Joyzelle say? . . . How she will laugh when she remembers her fears, for she imagined . . . No, she herself shall tell you what she thought, to punish her for her senseless terror . . . She used to hate you, but with a softened hatred that already smiled like one about to be pierced by the rays of love . . . But where is she hiding? . . . I have been seeking her for nearly two hours in vain . . . Have you seen her? I must tell her at once of the unspeakable happiness which this evening has brought us . . .

MERLIN

Not yet. I must remain in her eyes, until the close of the day, the pitiless tyrant whom she curses in her heart. My poor, dear child! . . . How I have tortured your adorable love! . . . But I have already told you the object of these proofs . . . In making you suffer, I have but been the instrument of fate and the unworthy slave of another will, whose source I do not know, which seems to demand that the slightest happiness should be surrounded by tears . . . I have but hastened, in order to bring happiness more quickly, the coming of those tears which hung in suspense between your two des-

tinies . . . You shall know some day by
what power, a power which has no magical or
supernatural quality, but which still lies hidden at the bottom of men's lives, I at times
command certain phenomena, certain appear-
ances that bewildered you. You shall also
learn that I have acquired the gift, often a
useless one, of reading the future a little
more clearly and a little further than the
rest of men . . . And so I saw you, groping
for each other, in time and space, for an unparalleled love, the most perfect perhaps that
the two or three centuries over which my eyes
have turned concealed within their shade . . .
You might have met each other after many
wanderings; but it was necessary to hasten
the expected meeting, because of you, my
son, whom death claimed in the absence of
love . . . And, on the other side, nothing
marked out Joyzelle for the hoped-for love,
save a few scattered and uncertain points
and the proofs themselves which she was to
surmount. I therefore hurried on the prescribed proofs: they have all been painful, but
necessary; the last will be decisive and more
serious . . .

Joyzelle

LANCÉOR

Serious? . . . What do you mean? . . .
It will not be dangerous for Joyzelle, or for
others? . . .

MERLIN

It will not be dangerous for Joyzelle, but
it imperils, for the last time, the predestined
love to which your life is linked . . . That
is why, despite of all, despite of my confidence, despite of my anticipations, my certainty even, I am afraid, I tremble a little at
the approach of the decisive hour . . .

LANCÉOR

If Joyzelle is to decide, love has nothing
to fear . . . Come, do not hesitate, Joyzelle
will always be the source of joy . . . But I
do not understand how, knowing the future,
you are not able to see her triumph beforehand? . . .

MERLIN

I already told you, before we came in here,
that Joyzelle can change the future which
she faces . . . She possesses a force which

113

I have seen in none save her; that is why I
do not know whether the great victory which
your love expects will not be mingled with
some little shadow and tears . . .

LANCÉOR

What do you mean? . . . You seem per-
turbed . . . What are you hiding from
me? . . . How can you believe that Joyzelle
would ever be the cause of a tear or the cause
of a shadow? . . . There is nothing in Joyzelle, not even the suffering which she might
inflict, there is nothing in her but brings
health, happiness and love! . . . Ah, how
well I see that you know little of the living triumph, the endless dawn contained in
her voice, her eyes, her heart! . . . One must
have held her in his arms to know what
treasures of hope, what torrents of certainty
issue from the least word murmured by her
lips, from the slightest smile that plays upon
her face . . . But I am too long delaying
the impatient victory. Go, father, go . . .
I will remain here, I will wait, I will watch
the happy moments pass, until my Joyzelle

utters a great cry of joy which shall tell me
that love has determined destiny . . .

> [Merlin *embraces* Lancéor *and goes*
> *out slowly.*]

SCENE II

(*The same room as in Act IV. The moon*
lights it with its blue radiance. On
the right, Merlin *is seated on the great*
marble bed. Arielle *is kneeling at the*
head of the bed, on the steps of the dais
that supports it.)

MERLIN

Arielle, the hour is striking and Joyzelle is
approaching . . . I have made the sacrifice
of my useless life; and yet I would that my
death, if possible, should not come to sadden
the most ardent and innocent love that the
world has known . . . But you tremble, you
weep, you hide from me your eyes swollen
with tears . . . What do you see, my child,
that you contemplate with so great a
dread? . . .

ARIELLE

Master, I beseech you, abandon this proof :
there is yet time! . . . My eyes cannot see
through the mist that surrounds it . . . It
may be mortal, I see it, I feel it ; and chance
has placed our two lives in the hand of a blind
and infatuated virgin . . . I do not want
to die! . . . There are other outlets . . . I
have always served you as your very thought
. . . But to-day I am afraid, I can follow
you no longer. . . . You well know that my
death is the echo of yours . . . Abandon
this : we will look elsewhere, in the future ; and
we can still escape the danger . . .

MERLIN

I cannot abandon the last proof . . . It
is for you to see that it does not turn to disaster. It is for you to grasp the as yet uncertain weapon which Joyzelle is preparing
to raise against us . . .

ARIELLE

But I do not know that I shall suc-
ceed! . . . Joyzelle's strength is so swift, so
profound, that it escapes my arm, escapes

116

my eyes, escapes destiny! . . . I see only the flash of falling steel . . . All is confused in a shadow; and my life and yours depend on a movement of my unskilful hand . . .

MERLIN

She is there, I hear her, she is feeling for the door . . . Be obedient and silent; I am obedient too. Watch and be quick and strong . . . I will close my eyes and await my fate . . .

ARIELLE

[*Dismayed and maddened.*] Abandon the proof! . . . I cannot go through with it! . . . I refuse! . . . I want to fly! . . .

MERLIN

[*Imperiously.*] Silence! . . . [*He stretches himself on the bed, closes his eyes and appears to be sleeping soundly. ARIELLE, overcome by her sobs, sinks down on the steps of the dais. On the left, at the opposite end of the room, a little door opens and JOYZELLE enters, wrapped in a long cloak and carrying a lamp in her hand. She takes two or three steps*

117

and stops. ARIELLE *rises and stands invisible behind the heavy curtains at the foot of the bed.*]

JOYZELLE

[*Stopping, haggard, hesitating, trembling.*] Now and here . . . I have taken the last step . . . Until this moment, which time can no longer keep back and which is about to see a thing that will never be wiped out; until I came to that little door which has just closed upon two captive destinies, I knew, I knew all that I had to do . . . Ah, I had reflected and I had judged so well! . . . There was nothing but that, there was nothing else: it was certain, it was just, it was inevitable! . . . But now all changes and I have forgotten all . . . There are other powers, there are other voices and I am all alone against all that speaks in the uncertain night . . . Justice, where are you? . . . Justice, what must I do? . . . I shall act because you wished it . . . You convinced me and urged me on . . . There, but now, under the thousands of stars which shone upon the door and which you invoked to reas-

sure my soul! . . . There was no doubt, then,
and all the certainty of all that breathes and
of all that quivers and of all that loves and
has a right to love illumined my heart! . . .
But, in face of the deed, you yourself draw
back, you deny your laws and abandon
me! . . . Ah, I feel too much alone, delivered like a blind slave to the unknown . . .
I shall walk without looking . . . I see nothing and I shall not raise my mad eyes to the
bed until the moment when the thing . . .
[*She advances with a mechanical step to the
foot of the bed.*] Now, fate itself shall say
yes . . . [*She lifts the lamp, looks at the
bed, sees* MERLIN *sleeping. and, in her surprise, takes a step back.*] He sleeps! . . .
what is this? . . . I had not foreseen . . .
Anything but this . . . Must I wait still?
. . . Oh, I should like to wait! . . . He is
sound asleep . . . Then he did not wish
. . . But, if he were not asleep, I could
not have done it . . . He would have disarmed me, he would have mastered me . . .
It must be true, it is fate, it is a good
and just fate that delivers him to me
thus . . . I, who was looking for a sign!

. . . But there is the sign! . . . What more do I want, if I want anything more? . . . . And yet, as he is asleep, I cannot know . . . Perhaps he has pity, perhaps he renounces and would bid me go! . . . He was not without soul; and often, at moments, he spoke like a father . . . Ah, if he had risen, if he had been there, with arms held out to me, in an attitude of . . . Then, then I should have been strong and should have conquered! . . . But a man asleep . . . That shatters hatred . . . And then, one no longer knows . . . And to change this sleep which one word puts to flight into that which no human or superhuman power can disturb! . . . Oh, I would at least that one word of forgiveness . . . Ah no, I am too great a coward! . . . This is terror seeking an outlet . . . I did not come for further meditation . . . There is no doubt, after what he did, after what he said! . . . I listen only to my voice, the voice of my destiny, which wills that I should save us both! . . . So much the worse if I am wrong! . . . I am right! I am right! . . . Go out, my lamp: I have seen all that

I need see . . . [*She puts out the lamp, places it on one of the marble stairs, seizes the dagger which she held concealed, raises it and looks at it for a moment.*] Now, it is your turn! . . . Ah, if you could do what my thought, my desperate pity wish, and if the death that gleams at the point of this blade were not real death, irrevocable death! . . . But enough . . . It is time . . . It is said, it is done, I strike! . . .

[*She raises the dagger to strike MER-LIN. ARIELLE, invisible, seizes her wrist and, without apparent effort, paralyses her gesture. At the same moment, MERLIN opens his eyes, smiling, rises and, with a movement of delight, takes JOY-ZELLE tenderly in his arms.*]

MERLIN

It is well! . . . Joyzelle is great and Joy-zelle triumphs! . . . She has conquered fate by listening to love; and it is you, my child, whom destiny marks out . . .

Joyzelle

[*Still failing to understand and struggling.*] No, no, no! . . . I could not . . . Ah, though my heart fail me, I have courage yet! . . . And I have all my life, if I no longer have my strength, and never, no, never, so long as I have breath . . .

MERLIN

Look at me, Joyzelle . . . I am restoring its strength to the arm which you raised in love's defence . . . I leave it its weapon which tried to strike me and which was striking true . . . Until that movement, all was undecided; now, all is clear, all is radiant and sure . . . Look at me, Joyzelle, and no longer fear my lips . . . They seek your brow, there at last to place the kiss which the father lays on the brow of his daughter . . .

JOYZELLE

What is this and what do you mean that I cannot understand? . . . Yes, I see in your eyes that you seem to love me as one loves a child . . . So I was mistaken and I was on the point of . . .?

Joyzelle

MERLIN

No, you were right; you would not have
been she whom love demands if you had not
done what you were going to do.

JOYZELLE

I do not know. I am dreaming . . . But
since it is not the abominable thing, I abandon myself to my dream . . .

MERLIN

Yes, it is true, my Joyzelle, I am yearning
to enjoy your delighted surprise, to follow your glances which seem to me so beautiful in their astonished flight, in which confidence dawns and which no longer know
where to rest their wings, like sea-birds that
have lost the shore . . . I am taking my
share of the happiness which I am bestowing
. . . I shall have no other . . . But do not
be anxious, we shall together enter into the
secrets of fate; and, when Lancéor . . .

JOYZELLE

Where is he?

Joyzelle

MERLIN

Ah, that name rouses you; and see, the
shore appears to those glances lost in space!
. . . Listen, I hear him . . . Your heart,
without our knowing it, has gone to tell him
that you loved him to the point which love
cannot surpass . . . He is hastening, he is
here! . . .

[*The door opens. Enter* LANCÉOR,
followed by ARIELLE, *invisible.*]

LANCÉOR

Father! . . . She is mine! . . .

MERLIN

My son, she has triumphed; destiny gives
her to you . . .

LANCÉOR

[*Taking* JOYZELLE *in his arms and covering her with wild kisses.*] Ah, I knew it
and I was sure of it! . . . Joyzelle, my
Joyzelle! . . . I do not ask what you can
have done to disarm fate . . . I know nothing yet; but we know all beforehand who
love each other as you and I love; and already

124

I hail the new truth that must have been
revealed at the first touch of your heart!
. . . Ah, father, father, I told you, I told
you! . . . But she does not understand why
I am embracing you . . . It is true, I go
too fast . . . Come here, Joyzelle, that I
may unite you both in my arms . . . We
had with us an enemy who loves us; he was
obliged to make us suffer; and that gentle
enemy was my own father, whom I thought
lost, my father here, my father found again,
who awaits but a smile to embrace you too
. . . Oh, do not turn away, do not look at
me with those eyes already laden with reproaches . . . I have hidden nothing from
you . . . I knew it to-day, this evening, the
moment you left me; and, so soon as I knew
it, I had to fly far from you, lest I should
betray myself, for all our happiness, it
appears, depended on this last secret; and,
when a secret is committed to love, it is as
though one hid a lighted lamp in a crystal
vase . . . You would have learnt all merely
by seeing my eyes, my hands, my very
shadow; and I could not show you my happiness . . . You were not to know of it till

125

the great proof ... It was necessary that
you should do an impossible thing ...
What thing I do not know; but, smile as
I might, I had to yield; I had to wait and
patiently count the minutes of the hour which
thus separated our two impatient pas-
sions ... But now, I hasten, I listen, I
want to know ... Speak, speak, I am
listening ...

JOYZELLE

Since you are happy, I am happy, too ...
I know nothing more ... I have scarce
awakened from a horrible and incomprehensible dream ...

MERLIN

Yes, my poor Joyzelle, the dream was horrible; but now it is overcome and the proof
is past, establishing a happiness which nothing threatens now, except the enemy that
threatens all men ...

LANCÉOR

But what, when all is told, was that
fearful proof? ...

Joyzelle

MERLIN

Joyzelle will tell you in the first kisses, free
from all anxiety, which you will exchange
after this victory. They will veil better than
my poor words what, in this proof, appears unpardonable . . . The proof was
dangerous and almost insurmountable . . .
Joyzelle could have chosen a different course
. . . She might have yielded, sacrificed herself, sacrificed her love, despaired, I know not
what! . . . She would not have been the Joyzelle that was expected . . . There was but
one path traced by destiny; she entered upon
it, followed it to the end and saved your life
in saving her own love . . .

JOYZELLE

It is ordained, then, that love strikes and
kills all that tries to bar its way? . . .

MERLIN

No, Joyzelle, I do not know . . . Let us
not make laws with a few scraps picked up in
the darkness that surrounds our thoughts
. . . But she who was to do what you were
willing to do was she whom fate intended

for my son . . . It was therefore written,
for you and for you alone and perhaps for
those who resemble you a little, that they have
a right to the love which fate points out to
them; and that that love must break down
injustice . . . I do not judge you: it is
fate that approves you; but I am overjoyed
that it has thus chosen you among all
women . . .

JOYZELLE

Father! . . . I tremble still when I see
that weapon which, for a moment . . . Forgive me, father, I loved you already . . .

MERLIN

It is I who ask you now to offer me a for-
giving hand . . .

JOYZELLE

No, no, these are not the cold hands of forgiveness! . . . These are the hands that
caress, worship and give thanks! . . . I
know now why, despite my hatred, I could not
hate! . . . What you have done was more
difficult than all that I have done, because it

was cruel; and, when I think again on what
has happened, it is you, it is you, father, who
have endured the heaviest and the most
deserving proof . . .

MERLIN

No, the most deserving was not among
those which you can discover . . . It will
remain the secret of this heart which loves
you both and unites you within itself and
which, to change this too-deep secret into
happiness, asks my two children for but a
moment of their joy and perhaps for a kiss
a little longer than those granted in passing
to old men whose time on earth is short . . .

LANCÉOR

[*Throwing himself in* MERLIN's *arms.*]
Father! . . .

JOYZELLE

[*Also embracing* MERLIN.] My father
too! . . .

ARIELLE

[*Trying to mingle with the closely entwined
group.*] No one sees me and no one thinks

129

of giving me my share of the love snatched
by my invisible hands from the miserly hands
of the days and years . . .

MERLIN

[*Smiling.*] I see you, Arielle: you love all
three of us; but a more ardent kiss ascends
towards Joyzelle than those which you give
to us . . . There, kiss her; the proof is
finished in my old heart too . . . Yet a little
while and we shall be far from her and far
from all love . . .

[ARIELLE *kisses* JOYZELLE *long and
slowly.*]

JOYZELLE

What are you saying, father, and to whom
are you speaking? . . . It seems as though
flowers which I cannot gather were lightly
touching my forehead and caressing my
lips . . .

MERLIN

Do not repel them, they are sad and
pure . . . It is my poor Arielle who spreads

them over you; it is my invisible daughter, the good fairy of the island, who discovered and protected you and Lancéor. She wishes to mingle, for the last time, in your great love and asks for a share, as discreet as herself, of the happiness which we owe her . . .

JOYZELLE

Where is she? . . . I see no one near me but you and Lancéor . . .

MERLIN

And do you think, my child, that we see all that lives deep down in our lives? . . . Be kind and gentle to poor Arielle . . . She is now giving you a parting kiss before going far away to disappear with me in the regions where fate wills that my destiny should be fulfilled . . .

LANCÉOR

To disappear with you? . . . Father, I do not know . . .

MERLIN

Let us not question those who have nothing

131

more to say . . . All is now determined
. . . Thanks to the unknown gods, I have
been able to give happiness to the two hearts
that were dearest to me; but I can do no more,
nor can you do anything, for my own happiness . . . I am going towards my destiny
and I go in silence, lest I should sadden this
smiling hour, which is yours alone . . . I
know what awaits me; and nevertheless I am
going . . .

JOYZELLE

No, no, no, no, father, you shall not
go! . . . We are around you and, if some
danger which we cannot see threatens your
old age, we shall try at least to alleviate the
dread of it . . . When there are three to
undergo a misfortune and those three love
one another, then the misfortune changes to
a burden of love, which we bear with delight . . .

MERLIN

Alas, no, my Joyzelle: it would all be useless! . . . Would to the gods that men had
to pass only through kindly evils, as yours

were! . . . But all life's secret purposes are not so clear, are not so good . . . But we speak in vain of what is written . . . I am still here, in the arms of those who love me . . . The day of my distress is not this day . . . Let us enjoy our hour, in the sweet sadness that follows on great joys, by listening to our minutes of love, passing and fleeting, one by one, in that frail ray of nocturnal light in which we clasp one another for our greater happiness . . . The rest does not as yet belong to men . . .

CURTAIN

APPENDIX I

(ACT III., SCENE II., *p.* 75). *If this trans-
figuration of* MERLIN'S *cannot be realised in a satisfactory manner on the
stage, it may be easily avoided by cut-
ting, on pp.* 77 *to* 81, *all that follows on*
JOYZELLE'S *exclamation. The scene will
then be as follows:*

JOYZELLE

[*Waking with a start.*] Lancéor! . . .
[*Recognising* MERLIN, *with a movement of
horror.*] You! . . .

MERLIN

Yes, it is I: the proof is grave and sad, etc.

(*The rest as on pp.* 81 *and* 85.)

APPENDIX II

(Act V., Scene II., *p.* 129). *Should there be
a fear of " tedious passages " (as Vil-
liers de L'isle-Adam said, " To be or not
to be," and generally speaking, all Ham-
let's speeches would be described to-day
as " tedious passages "), the* dénoue-
ment *could be hastened on, beginning
with* Arielle's *speech* (*p.* 129), *as
follows:*

ARIELLE

[*Who has remained standing at the foot
of the bed; in a sad and solemn voice.*]
Master!

MERLIN

I see you, Arielle, and I will obey . . .

JOYZELLE

What are you saying, father, and to whom
are you speaking?

136

Appendix

MERLIN

To her who opened up to you the road to happiness. She is now giving you a parting kiss, which I also give you . . .

JOYZELLE

A parting kiss?

LANCÉOR

Father!

JOYZELLE

What does this mean and what has happened?

MERLIN

Let us not question those who have nothing more to say. Would to the gods that, etc

(*The rest as in* MERLIN's *final speech.*)

THE END

MONNA VANNA

TRANSLATOR'S NOTE

This version of " Monna Vanna " advances
no claim to absolute literalness. It has been
prepared for stage presentation; and certain
expressions, perfectly inoffensive in the orig-
inal, have been modified, brought into line
with English ways of speech. There are
words in our language that, to use Mr. Mere-
dith's phrase, " for the sake of dignity, blush
to be named," and such blushes may fitly be
spared when a paraphrase is ready to hand.
It remains only to be said that M. Maeterlinck's work, pure and lofty throughout, has
been altered only at most immaterial points;
and that no alteration whatever has been
made without the full approval of the author.

CHARACTERS

GUIDO COLONNA, *Commander of the Pisan garrison*

MARCO COLONNA, *Guido's father*

PRINZIVALLE, *General in the pay of Florence*

TRIVULZIO, *Commissioner of the Florentine Republic*

TORELLO,
BORSO, } *Guido's lieutenants*

VEDIO, *Secretary to Prinzivalle*

GIOVANNA (MONNA VANNA), *Guido's wife*

PERIOD—*The end of the Fifteenth Century*

The first and third Acts take place in Pisa; the second outside the city

142

ACT I

A Room in the Palace of GUIDO COLONNA

(GUIDO *and his lieutenants,* BORSO *and* TOR-
ELLO, *are standing by an open window,
from which there is a view of the country
around Pisa.*)

GUIDO

O UR present extremity is so great that
the Seigniory have been compelled to
reveal to me disasters they had long kept
back. The two armies that Venice despatched
to our relief are both hemmed in by the
Florentines; the one at Bibbiena, the other at
Elci. Chiusi, Montalone, the passes of the
Vernia, Arezzo, and the defiles of the Casentine—these are all held by the enemy. We
are isolated and helpless, given over to the
hatred of Florence; and Florence is unfor-
giving when she no longer trembles. Our
soldiers, the people, are still unaware of these

disasters, but strange rumours are afoot, and daily becoming more definite. What will the Pisans do, when they learn the truth? Their rage will turn upon us, upon the Seigniory; we shall be the first to fall victim to their terror and blind despair. They have endured so much, during this long siege, that has lasted more than three months; they have borne their suffering so heroically, that it need not surprise us if famine and misery goad them now to madness. One hope was left to them; that is gone, and, with it, the last vestige of our authority. We shall be powerless. The enemy will batter down our walls, and Pisa cease to be . . .

BORSO

My men have shot their last arrow; their ammunition is spent. One may search the vaults from end to end without finding an ounce of powder . . .

TORELLO

We fired our last cannon ball two days ago at the batteries of Sant' Antonio; and even the Stradiotes, who now have nothing left but

their swords, refuse to man the ramparts . . .

BORSO

From this window the breach can be seen
that Prinzivalle's cannon have made in our
walls . . . It is fifty paces wide; a flock of
sheep could pass through . . . The place is
untenable; and the Romagnians, the Scla-
vonians, and the Albanians have signified their
intention to desert in a body should the capitulation not be signed to-night . . .

GUIDO

Thrice within the last ten days have the
Seigniory sent ancients of the College to treat
for capitulation. These have none of them
returned . . .

TORELLO

Prinzivalle does not forgive us the murder
of his lieutenant, Antonio Reno, whom the
frenzied peasants hacked to death in our
streets. Florence avails herself of this murder to proclaim us outside the law, and treat
us as barbarians . . .

Monna Vanna

I have sent my own father to Prinzivalle
to express our profound regret, and explain
how powerless we were to control a mob
whom hunger had driven frantic.   My father
was a sacred hostage.   He has not yet returned . . .

For more than a week now the city has lain
open, and exposed on every side; our walls
are a mass of ruin, our cannon silent.   Why
does Prinzivalle not give the order for
assault?   Can it be that his courage has
failed him, or does he dread some ambush?
Florence, perhaps, may have sent mysterious
orders . . .

The orders of Florence are ever mysterious, but her designs are clear.   Pisa, by her
unswerving loyalty to Venice, has set a
dangerous example to the little Tuscan cities;
the Republic of Pisa, therefore, must cease
to be . . . Florence has displayed rare artifice and cunning.   She has contrived, little
by little, to embitter this war, to poison it
with strange acts of treachery and cruelty,

146

that shall be held to warrant her pitiless revenge. It is not without cause that I suspect her emissaries of having incited our peasants to massacre Reno. So, too, was it part of her scheme to entrust this siege to Prinzivalle, the most barbarous mercenary in her employ—the man who won for himself such sinister fame at the sack of Placenza, where he put every man who bore arms to the sword—though he declared later this was done against his orders!—and sold five thousand free women into slavery . . .

BORSO

Such is the report, I know, but it is not correct. It was not Prinzivalle, but the Florentine Commissioners, who were responsible both for the massacre and the sale. I have never seen Prinzivalle, but one of my brothers knew him well. He is of barbarian origin. His father would seem to have been a Basque or a Breton, who kept a goldsmith's shop in Venice. He is undoubtedly of humble birth, but still not the savage that people hold him. From what I hear he is a dangerous creature, of dissolute habits, fantastic and violent, but,

for all that, loyal; and I would unhesitatingly
hand him my sword . . .

GUIDO

Wait till your arm can no longer wield it!
And very soon now he will be stirring, and
show us what he is! In the meanwhile we
have one chance left: such of us, at least, as
dare to meet death bravely, and to look it in
the face . . . We must tell the whole truth
to the soldiers, the citizens, and the peasants
who have found shelter in our walls. They
shall learn that no offer of capitulation has
been made to us; and that we have not here
one of those mimic wars in which two great
armies fight from dawn to sunset, leaving
three wounded on the field; not a fraternal
siege that ends by the victor becoming the
guest and the cherished friend of the van-
quished. This is a bitter struggle for life
or death; a struggle in which no mercy is
shown; in which our wives and our children . . .

[*Enter* MARCO. GUIDO *sees him and
rushes eagerly to embrace him.*]

GUIDO

Father! . . . By what happy miracle, what stroke of good fortune in this calamity of ours, have you been restored to us, when I had almost given up hope . . . You are not wounded? You drag your foot behind you! Have they tortured you? How did you escape? What have they done to you?

MARCO

Nothing. They are not barbarians, thank God! They received me as an honoured guest. Prinzivalle had read my works; he spoke to me of the three dialogues of Plato, that I had found and translated. I am lame, it is true, but then I had far to go, and I am very old . . . Do you know whom I met in Prinzivalle's tent?

GUIDO

The merciless Commissioners from Florence!

MARCO

Yes, they were there—or, at least, one of them, for I saw only one . . . But the first

name I heard was that of Marsilio Ficino, the
man who revealed Plato to the world . . .
Plato would seem to live again in Marsilio
Ficino . . . I would have given ten years of
my life to see him, before going whither all
must go . . . We were like two brothers
who had come together at last . . . We
spoke of Hesiod, of Homer, Aristotle . . .
Close to the camp, beside the banks of the
Arno, he had unearthed, in a grove of olive,
the torso of a goddess that had lain buried in
the sand: it was so strangely beautiful that
if you saw it you would forget the war. We
dug on a little further; he found an arm, and
I two hands . . . These hands were so pure,
so delicate, they held such a radiant happiness, that one fancied them formed for
naught else than to scatter the dew, or
caress the dawn . . . One was curved tenderly, as though it had lain against a woman's
breast; the other still clasped the handle of
a mirror . . .

GUIDO

Father, father! Let us not forget that,
here, people are perishing of hunger, and

have little to do with delicate hands, or bronze
torsos!

MARCO

This one is of marble . . .

GUIDO

Be it so! But let us speak rather of the
thirty thousand lives to whom a moment's
delay, a single imprudent act, spells ruin;
whereas a word could save them: a whisper
of good news . . . It was not for a torso
or a mutilated hand that you went yonder!
What did they say to you? What designs has Florence, or Prinzivalle? Tell us
quickly! Why do they dally with us? Do
you hear those cries underneath our window? The poor wretches are fighting for the
grass that has grown between the stones . . .

MARCO

You are right. I was forgetting that men
were at war with each other now that spring
is here, and the glad sky smiling upon the
earth, and the sea stretching towards the blue
like a radiant cup that a goddess presents to
the gods of heaven; and the earth so fair and

so full of love for men! . . . But you have
your joys; I dwell too long on mine . . .
Besides, you are right. I should have told
you at once the news that I bring . . . I
bear a message fraught with salvation to
thirty thousand lives, and with heavy afflic-
tion to one . . . But this one may find
therein most noble occasion for glory, of a
kind that seems greater to me than all the
glories of war . . . Love for one person is
good, and brings its own happiness; but the
love that enfolds the many is greater and
finer still . . . The virtues that all men admire are good; yet there come days when our
eye travels beyond them, and then their value
seems less . . . Listen! . . . And prepare
yourself for what I have to say, lest my first
words should wring from you one of those
oaths that bar our retreat, and enchain the
reason that fain would retrace her steps . . .

GUIDO

[*Dismissing his officers with a gesture.*]
Leave us!

MARCO

No! Remain . . . It is our fate, the fate

of us all, that we are about to decide! Indeed, I could wish that this room overflowed with the victims whom we shall save! That all the poor wretches to whom we bring comfort might be at the window there, to hear and retain for ever the tidings I bring; for I bring salvation, if reason will but accept it! Nor could ten thousand reasons turn the scale against one overpowering error, whereof I fear the weight the more, inasmuch as I myself . . .

GUIDO

Have done with enigmas, father, I entreat you! What can this matter be that calls for so many words? Tell us all! There is nothing can frighten us now!

MARCO

Be it so, then! Listen! I saw Prinzivalle; I have had speech with him . . . It is strange how false is the picture men draw of one whom they hold in dread . . . I went to him as Priam to the tent of Achilles. I thought to meet a drunken, bloodstained savage—a madman whose only quality was a certain talent for war . . . For as such had he always been represented to me . . . I expected to find the incarnate fiend of battle, headstrong and incoherent, vain, debauched, treacherous, cruel . . .

GUIDO

And all this is Prinzivalle, save that he be no traitor!

BORSO

Nay, traitor he is not; and, though he serve Florence, his loyalty is unstained . . .

MARCO

The man I met bowed down before me as though he were my disciple, and I the master whom he revered. He is learned, studious, wise, eager in search of knowledge. He listens patiently, and his eyes are open to all things that are beautiful. He is humane and generous, and has no liking for war; he is conscientious and sincere, the reluctant servant of a perfidious Republic. The hazards of life—destiny, it may be—made him a soldier, and hold him captive still to a glory that he detests, and fain would abandon, but not before he has gratified a desire; a fearful desire, such as would seem to fall on some men who are born beneath the perilous star of a great, unique, and unrealisable love . . .

GUIDO

Father, father, you forget that men who are dying of hunger can ill brook this delay! What are this man's qualities to us? You spoke of salvation; give us the word you promised!

MARCO

It is true. I do wrong to hesitate; for cruel as this thing may be to the two creatures I love best of all on this earth . . .

GUIDO

My share I accept, though it be what it may; but who is the other?

MARCO

Listen, I will . . . As I entered this room it seemed strange and difficult to me; and yet the chance of salvation was so overwhelming . . .

GUIDO

Speak!

Monna Vanna

Florence is determined on our annihilation.
The decemvirs of war have judged it necessary, the Seigniory have approved their
decree; the decision is irrevocable. But
Florence is too prudent, too wise in her hypocrisy, to allow the world that she is civilising
to lay the charge of indiscriminate bloodshed
at her door. She will declare, therefore, that
we refused the merciful capitulation she had
offered. The city will be taken by assault;
Spanish and German mercenaries will be
hurled against her. And these need no urg-
ing, when there is chance of pillage or burn-
ing, of rapine or slaughter! A mere matter
of slipping the muzzle: and the leaders, that
day, will take care to seem helpless, to have
lost all control . . . Such is the fate held in
store for us; and the city of the red lily will
be the first to deplore the disaster, and will
ascribe it wholly to the unforeseen licence of
the foreign mercenaries, whom she will dis-
band with every expression of horror, so
soon as our ruin shall enable her to dispense
with their services . . .

GUIDO

Yes. That is the way of Florence . . .

MARCO

These are the private instructions that
Prinzivalle has received from the Commissioners of the Republic. Day after day,
through this last week, they have urged him
to deliver the final assault. Hitherto he has
delayed it under various pretexts. Further,
he has intercepted letters wherein the Commissioners, who spy upon his every movement, accuse him of treachery to the Seigniory. Pisa destroyed, and the war over, con-
demnation, torture, and death await him in
Florence, as they have awaited more than
one dangerous general. So that he knows
his fate . . .

GUIDO

Very well then, what does he propose?

MARCO

He is certain—as far, at least, as one can
be certain where these shiftly savages are concerned—of a fair proportion of the archers,

whom he himself enrolled.   But, in any event,
he has a bodyguard of a hundred men, who
are devoted to him; and on these he can
absolutely rely.   His proposal is that all who
may choose to follow him shall be brought
into Pisa, and help to defend her against the
army he will abandon . . .

GUIDO

It is not men we need; and these dangerous
auxiliaries do not tempt us.   Let him give us
bullets, provisions, powder.

MARCO

He foresaw that his offer might appear
suspicious to you, and perhaps be rejected.
He will undertake, therefore, to pass into the
city a convoy of three hundred waggons,
laden with ammunition and food, that have
just entered his camp.

GUIDO

How can he do this?

MARCO

I know not.   The ways of war and politics
are strange to me.   But he does what he

will . . . The Florentine Commissioners notwithstanding, he is absolute master in his
camp so long as the Seigniory have not removed him from his command. And this
they dare not do on the eve of victory, in the
midst of an army that has faith in him, and
already clutches its prey. Florence must
wait her hour!

GUIDO

Good, I understand; he saves us that he
may save himself. He seeks revenge. But
this, I imagine, could be achieved in other
fashions, and more skilfully too. What can
his interest be in saving his enemies?
Whither will he go, and what will become of
him? What does he demand in return?

MARCO

The moment has come, my son, when words
turn cruel and all-powerful, when two or
three syllables suddenly borrow the force of
destiny, and fasten upon their victims . . .
I tremble when I think that the sound of my
voice, the way in which I may say what has
to be said, can cause so many deaths, or save
so many lives . . .

Monna Vanna

Why do you hesitate? . . . The cruellest words can add nothing to such a misfortune as ours . . .

MARCO

I have told you that Prinzivalle seems wise; that he is reasonable, humane . . . But where is the man so wise as to have no moment of folly; so virtuous as never to have harboured some monstrous idea within him? . . . Are not our reason, our pity and justice, for ever at war with desire, with passion, with the madness that lies so near to our soul? . . . I, myself, have succumbed more than once, and I shall again, and so, perhaps, will you . . . For it happens thus with us all! A sorrow awaits you that should be no sorrow perhaps, could you consider it rightly . . . And I who see so clearly that this sorrow is out of all proportion to the wrong that will cause it, I, for my part, have made a promise still more foolish than is this foolish sorrow . . . And my foolish promise will be foolishly kept by the sage I fain would be; the sage who ventures to speak in the

name of reason . . . Should you reject this
offer, I have undertaken to return to the
enemy's camp . . . And what will await
me there? Death and torture will probably be the reward of my absurd loyalty
. . . And none the less I shall go . . . Tell
myself as I may that I am merely trick-
ing out folly in purple that I may delude
myself, I still shall do the foolish thing I
deplore; for I, also, lack the strength that
he must possess who would listen to reason
alone . . . But I have not yet told you.
Ah, see how I lose my thread, how I weave
phrase after phrase, pile word upon word, to
retard, be it ever so little, the moment that
must decide! But I wrong you, perhaps,
by my doubts . . . See them! This mighty
convoy that my own eyes have beheld; these
waggons laden with corn and wine and fruit;
these flocks of sheep and herds of cattle,
enough, and more than enough, to feed a
people for weeks; these barrels of powder and
bars of lead with which Florence may be overcome and prosperity brought back to Pisa;
all these shall be introduced this very night
into our city if you will send in exchange and

deliver to Prinzivalle—and she shall return with the first rays of dawn—but he demands, in token of victory and submission, that she come alone, and clad only in her mantle. . . .

GUIDO

Who? Who is to go? You have not told me . . .

MARCO

Giovanna.

GUIDO

What! My wife? . . . Vanna? . . .

MARCO

Yes, your Vanna . . . At last I have said it!

GUIDO

But, why Vanna? Are there not a thousand women?

MARCO

It is because she is the most beautiful, and he loves her . . .

GUIDO

He loves her! . . . Where has he seen her? He does not know her!

MARCO

He has seen her. He knows her, but would
not say when or how . . .

GUIDO

But she, has she seen him? Where have
they met?

MARCO

She has never seen him, or, at least, she
does not remember . . .

GUIDO

How do you know this?

MARCO

She told me herself . . .

GUIDO

What!

MARCO

Before I came here to you . . .

GUIDO

And you told her?

MARCO

All . . .

163

Monna Vanna

GUIDO

What! you cannot have dared to hint at
this infamous bargain?

MARCO

Yes . . .

GUIDO

And she said? . . .

MARCO

Nothing . . . Her face grew white: she
left me . . .

· GUIDO

Ah, she did well! . . . That was better
perhaps than loading you with reproaches,
and throwing herself at your feet . . . Yes,
that was better . . . She turned white and
left you . . . So would an angel have done;
that is like Vanna . . . What was there to
say? Nothing! And we, too, shall say
nothing . . . Come, my friends, we will return to the ramparts, and die, at least, since
die we must, without staining ourselves with
dishonour . . .

MARCO

Ah, Guido, the ordeal is terrible, I know!

164

Monna Vanna

Now that the blow has fallen let us be patient, and give reason time to discriminate between duty and private sorrow! . . .

GUIDO

Duty! My duty is clear. Your monstrous offer entails one duty on me, and one duty alone. I need no time to reflect.

MARCO

And yet must you ask yourself whether you have a right to sacrifice a whole people; whether thousands of lives be not too high a price to pay . . . Did your happiness alone depend on this choice I could understand your preferring death; though to me who am near the end of life—to me who have seen many men and therefore much human sorrow, to me there can be no moral or physical evil that is not preferable to death, cold and horrible death, with its eternal silence . . . And here many thousands of lives are at stake; here your brothers in arms are concerned, their wives and children! . . . If you yield to a madman's frenzy, then the thing that seems monstrous to you shall be

called heroic by those who come after. For
they will judge with calmer eyes, with more
justice, and more humanity . . . Believe me,
nothing can equal the saving of life. Virtues,
ideals, all that we know as honour and loyalty,
are mere trifles compared with that . . .
You would seek to pass through this ordeal
like a hero, unstained; but it is wrong to
believe that death is the loftiest peak of heroism . . . The most heroic deed is the one
that costs us most, and death is often far
easier than life . . .

GUIDO

Are you my father?

MARCO

Yes, and proud to be your father . . . In
opposing you to-day I oppose myself also,
and I should love you less did you submit
too readily . . .

GUIDO

Yes, you are my father, you have given
your proof; for you, too, shall choose death
for your share; and since I reject this loathsome compact, you shall return to the enemy's

camp, and there meet the fate that Florence
reserves for you . . .

MARCO

My son, here I alone am concerned—a
feeble and useless old man, with few years to
live, a man of no value to any—and therefore
did I tell myself that I might still humour an
ancient folly, nor struggle to do what I know
should be done if one indeed sought to be
wise . . . I know not why I shall go yonder . . . My soul has remained too young
in this old body of mine; and I belong to a
time in which reason had little to say . . .
But I regret that so many influences of the
past should keep me from breaking a foolish
promise . . .

GUIDO

I shall act like you . . .

MARCO

What do you mean?

GUIDO

I shall follow your example. I, too, shall
remain faithful to those influences of the past

that you now regard as absurd, though you
fortunately still permit them to regulate
your conduct . . .

MARCO

Where others are concerned I cast them
from me; and since it appears that your
soul demands my encouragement, demands
the poor sacrifice of my word, then I renounce in my heart the fulfilment of my
promise, and come what may, and decide
as you will, I shall not return yonder . . .

GUIDO

Enough! There are things a son must not
say to an erring father . . .

MARCO

Say what you would, my son: let your in-
dignant words flow freely from your heart
. . . I shall regard them as the token of your
most legitimate grief . . . Words cannot
alter my love for you . . . But, while curs-
ing me, let reason and gentle pity take the
place in your soul of the maledictions that
leave it . . .

168

Monna Vanna

GUIDO

Enough: I will hear no more . . . Think; and try to consider what it is you would have me do. For at this moment it is you who are lacking in reason, in noble and lofty reason; you whose wisdom is troubled by the fear of death . . . Death does not frighten me . . . I can still remember the time when you enjoined courage upon me, before your own was weakened by age and the vain study of books . . . We are alone in this room. No one has beheld your pitiful weakness; and my two lieutenants and I will keep the secret that we shall, alas, not have to keep very long! We shall bury all this in our hearts; and now let us turn our thoughts to the final struggle . . .

MARCO

Nay, my son, buried it cannot be; for years, and the studies that you deem so vain, have taught me that it can never be right, whatever the reason, to bury the life of a single man; and though I indeed should no longer possess the courage that alone finds favour in your eyes, I still have another, less dazzling, perhaps, less highly esteemed by

men, since it achieves less, and men admire
most that which brings suffering to them
. . . This will enable me to accomplish the
rest of my duty . . .

GUIDO

And what may that duty be?

MARCO

I shall complete what I have so unsuc-
cessfully begun . . . You were one of the
judges, but not the only judge; and all those
whose life or death hangs on this hour have a
right to know their fate, and to be told upon
what their salvation depends . . .

GUIDO

I do not understand you.   At least, I hope
I do not.   You were saying . . .

MARCO

That on leaving this room I shall at once
inform the people of the offer that Prinzivalle
has made and you have rejected . . .

GUIDO

It is well!   Now I understand.   I regret

that idle words should have brought us to this, as I regret also that your delusions should compel me to be wanting in the respect that is due to your age . . . But it is a son's duty to protect a deluded father against himself; and while Pisa stands I am master here, and the custodian of her honour . . . Borso and Torello, I entrust my father to your care, until such time as his conscience shall reawaken within him. Nothing has happened! . . . No one shall know . . . Father, I forgive you; and you will forgive me, too, when, at the last hour, you remember how you once taught me to become master of myself, and unafraid . . .

MARCO

I have no need to wait for the last hour in order to forgive you, my son . . . I should have acted like you . . . And you may imprison me, but not my secret; for that is free, and can no longer be stifled . . .

GUIDO

What is this? What is this you say?

MARCO

That at this very moment Prinzivalle's proposal is being discussed by the Seigniory . . .

GUIDO

The Seigniory! Who can have told them?

MARCO

I told them before I came here . . .

GUIDO

You! No. No, it is impossible! However great your fear, or the havoc that age has wrought in your heart, you cannot have delivered the one joy of my soul, my love, the purity and beauty of our wedded life, into the hands of strangers, of miserable shopkeepers, who would weigh it and measure it as though it were salt or oil! . . . I cannot believe it. . . . I shall not, till my own eyes have seen it . . . And then I shall look upon you, you the father whom I loved and thought I knew, whom I took as my model, I shall look on you with no less horror and hatred than I do on the vile and cowardly monster who has besmirched us to-day with all this infamy!

Monna Vanna

MARCO

You speak truly, my son. You do not
know me; and for that I am to blame. When
old age came upon me I did not tell you what
I learned from it every day concerning life,
and love, and the joys and sorrows of men
. . . Had I acquainted you sooner with all
that was passing in my heart, with all the
vanities that were slowly departing, and the
truths that were taking their place, then
should I not be standing before you to-day
like some unhappy stranger whom you are
beginning to hate . . .

GUIDO

'At least I rejoice that I did know you
sooner . . . And as for the rest . . . it is
not difficult to foretell what the Seigniory will
decide. To save themselves they have only to
sacrifice one man, and that is so simple! Such
a temptation would force a nobler courage
than one has the right to expect from these
poor traders. And yet, let them beware!
That is asking too much. That is more than
they have a right to ask. I have shed my
blood for them; by day and by night have I

toiled and endured; through this whole long siege I have never spared myself. But that is enough: and I will do no more! Vanna is mine! She belongs to me, and I am yet in command! My Stradiotes will at least remain faithful; I have three hundred men who will listen to me alone, and turn a deaf ear to the counsels of cowards!

MARCO

You are in error, my son. The Seigniory of Pisa, the citizens whom you speak of so slightingly, before even knowing what their decision may be, have in this crisis given proof of an admirable nobility and courage. They have refused to owe their safety to the sacrifice of a woman's love; and as I left them and hastened to you, they were summoning Vanna, to tell her that they placed in her hands the fate of the city . . .

GUIDO

What! They have dared! In my absence, they have dared to repeat to her the foul words of that loathsome satyr! . . . My Vanna! . . . When I think of her tender

174

face, that fires at a glance—of the shrinking
modesty that makes her beauty lovelier still
—my Vanna to have stood before these
lecherous old men, these little pale-faced
hypocritical traders, who have always looked
upon her as something holy! " Go," they
will have said to her, " go yonder, naked and
alone, to the barbarian's tent! Do his bidding!" Ah, truly, it was noble indeed of
them to have used no violence! They knew
that I am still here. They ask *her* consent,
you say! And mine—who will dare ask
mine?

MARCO

Have I not done so, my son? And if you
refuse me they will come in their turn . . .

GUIDO

Let them! Vanna will have spoken for us
both . . .

MARCO

I trust that it may be so, and that you will
accept her answer . . .

GUIDO

Her answer! Can you doubt it, you who

175

know her, who have seen her every day
since the one when, with smiles of love in her
eyes, she first crossed the threshold of this
very room, in which now you wish to sell her?
You doubt her answer? . . .

MARCO

My son, each of us sees only in others what
he sees in himself, and knows himself only to
the extent of his own consciousness . . .

GUIDO

That is doubtless why I knew you so ill!
But rather than that these eyes of mine should
a second time be so cruelly deceived, I would
pray God that they be closed for ever!

MARCO

They may be about to open, my son, beneath a very great light . . . I say this because I have noticed a certain strength in
Vanna that you have not seen, and it is this
that leaves me in no doubt as to what her
reply will be . . .

GUIDO

You have no doubt! Ah, believe me,
neither have I! And I accept her reply in

advance, blindly, irrevocably! If it be not
the same as mine, then have we both been deceived in each other, from the very first hour
unto this one of sorrow . . . And our love
will have been a mere lie, that now crumbles
to dust; and all I adored in her will have
existed only in this poor credulous head of
mine, in this poor faithful heart that knew of
one happiness only and worshipped a phantom . . .

> [*Cries of " Vanna, Vanna," arise from
> the crowd outside, at first as a mur-
> mur, and then growing louder and
> louder. The door, at back, opens,
> and* VANNA, *alone and pale, ad-
> vances into the room, while men
> and women, who seem afraid to
> enter, try to hide themselves against
> the door.* GUIDO *sees her, and
> rushes towards her. He throws his
> arms round her and embraces her
> feverishly.*]

GUIDO

My Vanna! . . . What have they done,
what have they said to you! . . . No, no, do
not tell me . . . I need only look into your

eyes—there all is still pure and loyal, like a
fountain that angels bathe in . . . Ah, those
foolish men! They could harm nothing of
what I loved; they have been like children
who throw stones in the air, and imagine they
can hit the sky . . . As they gazed into
your eyes their words will have shrivelled on
their lips . . . You had no need to answer
—you will merely have looked at them . . .
And then, between them and you, between
their thoughts and yours, a lake will have
sprung up, a limitless ocean of life and love
. . . But see, there is one here, a man whom
I call father . . . He sinks his head; his
white hairs hide it . . . We must forgive
him; he is old and blinded. We must be
merciful; we must make a great effort; your
eyes say nothing to him—he is so far from
us! . . . He has become a stranger; our love
has passed over his sad old age like an April
shower that falls upon flints . . . Our love
is nothing to him; it has all escaped him
. . . He thinks that we love as they do who
know not what the word means . . . He
cannot understand, he needs words . . .
Give him words; give him your answer!

Monna Vanna

VANNA

[*Approaching* MARCO.] My father, I shall go to-night.

MARCO

[*Kissing her brow.*] My daughter, I know . . .

GUIDO

What! What do you say?

VANNA

Guido, I shall go. I must; I must obey . . .

GUIDO

Obey? Obey whom? Tell me!

VANNA

I shall go to Prinzivalle's tent to-night . . .

GUIDO

To die with him, to kill him? That had not occurred to me. Yes, yes, I can understand that!

VANNA

Were I to kill him our city would not be saved . . .

179

Monna Vanna

GUIDO

What! You, you love him then! Since
when do you love him?

VANNA

I do not know him; I have never seen
him . . .

GUIDO

But you have heard. Yes, yes, you have
heard, people have told you . . .

VANNA

Nothing. Some one said just now that he
was a very old man . . .

GUIDO

He is not! He is young, he is handsome,
much younger than I. God! had he asked
anything else I would have gone to him,
crawled on my hands and knees, to save our
city! Or wandered away with her and spent
the rest of our life, unknown and forgotten,
begging for alms at the cross-roads! . . .
But this, this! Never in the history of the
world has a conqueror dared— [*Going to*
VANNA *and flinging his arms round her.*]

Ah, Vanna, my Vanna, I cannot believe it! It is not your voice that I heard, but my father's and his alone! No, I have heard nothing; all is as it was . . . You shall tell me that I am mistaken, that your love, that all that was you, cried out, " No, no! " ashamed even at having to speak! . . . I tell you I have heard nothing, nothing; the silence has been unbroken . . . But, see, now you must speak . . . All are listening . . . No one has heard . . . All are waiting for the word you must say . . . Say it quickly, Vanna, that they may know you! Quickly! Declare our love, and dispel this dream . . . Speak the word I wait for, the word that must be spoken if all things are not to crumble in ruins around me! . . .

VANNA

O Guido, I know how hard it must be to bear . . .

GUIDO

[*Instinctively thrusting her from him.*] How hard it must be! You know, you know? Have I not to bear it all, I who loved? You never have loved me! No, I begin to see!

What am I to make of all this? . . . You are
glad to leave me; you love this man, who
knows! Ah, but here I still am the master,
say what they will! . . . And you think I
shall stand calmly by and let these things be?
Beneath this room is a dungeon, a dark, cold
dungeon, and there you shall stay while my
Stradiotes keep watch, until such time as your
heroism shall have cooled, and you learn
where your duty lies . . . Take her away!
. . . I have spoken; it is my command! Go,
and obey!

VANNA

Guido, Guido, I need surely not tell
you . . .

GUIDO

They do not obey! No one here to do my
bidding! You, Borso, Torello, have your
arms turned to stone? Can my voice not
make itself heard! . . . You, down there,
you others, who stand and listen, can you not
hear me? I shout to them; they do not move
. . . Take her away, I say! . . . Away,
away! . . . Ah, I see what it is! They are
afraid; they want to live—to live, that is all
they care for! I must die that they may

live; but not that way! . . . No, no, that
were surely too easy . . . Here am I alone
against the crowd, and I am to pay for it
all . . . Why I, and not you! You all
have wives! . . . [*Half drawing his sword
and approaching* VANNA.] And what if I
prefer death to dishonour? . . . That had
not occurred to you! . . . But, see, I have
only to raise my hand——

VANNA

If your love bids you, Guido . . .

GUIDO

" If your love bids you "! Ah, yes, speak
of love, you who never have known what it
means! You, in whose soul there can never
have been any love! Now as I look at you I
see a desert—a desert where all is swallowed
up, parched and dying . . . not even a tear,
not a tear! . . . What was I, what was I to
you? A man whose arms offered shelter,
that was all! . . . Had you but for an
instant . . .

VANNA

Guido, look at me, look at me! Can you

183

not see? What shall I say to you, Guido?
Have I words to tell what I feel? Let me
speak but one single word and all my strength
goes! . . . I cannot . . . I love you, I owe
everything to you! . . . And yet I shall go;
I must, I must . . .

GUIDO

[*Thrusting her from him.*] It is well!
Go; get you hence! Go to him, I give you
up. Go! You are mine no longer . . .

VANNA

[*Seizing his hand.*] Guido! . . .

GUIDO

[*Pushing her away.*] Ah, do not clutch
at me with those warm, soft hands . . . My
father was right; he knew you better . . .
Father, here she is. This is your work, finish
it now to the end . . . Lead her to this man's
tent. I shall stay here and watch you go off
together . . . But do not imagine that I
claim a share in the bread and meat she will
buy . . . There remains but one thing for
me, and that you shall know very soon . . .

184

Monna Vanna

[*Clinging to him.*] Guido, look at me;
do not turn your eyes from me—that is
too dreadful . . . Let me see your eyes,
Guido . . .

GUIDO

See then! Look into my eyes, and read
. . . Go, I know you no longer! Time
presses—out yonder he waits: night is falling . . . Go! what have you to fear? I
shall not kill myself. I am not mad; it is
only when love is triumphant that reason
totters, not when love crumbles . . . I have
gazed into the very depths of love, ay,
of love and fidelity . . . I have no more to
say. No, no, unclasp your fingers; they cannot detain a vanishing love. All is over,
finished, done with; there remains not a trace!
. . . The past is engulfed, and the future
too . . . Ah, yes, those pure white fingers,
those noble eyes, those lips; there was a time
when I believed . . . Now nothing remains
. . . [*Casting* VANNA's *hands from him.*]
Nothing, nothing, less than nothing! Farewell, Vanna! Get you gone. Farewell . . .
You go yonder? . . .

Monna Vanna

Yes . . .

GUIDO

You will not return? . . .

VANNA

Yes, I shall return . . .

GUIDO

As to that, we shall see . . . Ah, we shall see . . . Who could have told me that my father knew her better than I! . . .

> [*He totters, and clings to one of the marble columns. *VANNA* goes out slowly and alone, without another glance at him.*]

ACT II

Prinzivalle's *Tent*

(Sumptuous disorder. Hangings of silk and gold. Arms and precious furs are strewn about the place. Great chests lie half open, revealing quantities of jewels and glittering stuffs. The entrance to the tent is from the back, through a heavy curtain. Prinzivalle, standing by a table, is arranging documents, plans, and arms. Enter Vedio.)

VEDIO

HERE is a letter from the Commissioner of the Republic.

PRINZIVALLE

From Trivulzio?

VEDIO

Yes. Messer Maladura, the second Commissioner, has not yet returned.

PRINZIVALLE

The Venetian army, that threatens Florence from the Casentine, is probably offering unexpected resistance. Give me the letter. [*He takes it and reads.*] He sends me the formal command, under penalty of immediate arrest, and for the very last time, to deliver the assault at dawn . . . It is well. The night, at least, is mine . . . Immediate arrest . . . Ah, how little they know! . . . Do they really imagine that stale, hackneyed words like these can bring terror to the man who awaits the unique hour of his life! . . . Threats, arrest, calumny, trial, judgment— what are all these to me? . . . They would have arrested me long ago, had they been able, had they dared . . .

VEDIO

Messer Trivulzio told me, as he gave me the letter, that he would follow. He desires to speak with you . . .

PRINZIVALLE

Ah, so he has made up his mind at last . . . Our interview will decide many things;

and this wizened little scribe, who stands here
for all the occult power of Florence, and yet
dares not raise his eyes to mine; this
wretched, pale-faced dwarf who hates me
more than death, shall spend an hour he has
not looked for . . . Grave orders must have
reached him that he ventures to beard the
monster in his den . . . What guards are
at my door?

VEDIO

Two old soldiers of your Galician band.
I thought I recognised Hernando, and the
other, I believe, is Diego.

PRINZIVALLE

Good; they would obey me, those two, did
I tell them to put all the saints of heaven in
chains . . . It is growing dark; have the
lamp lit.   What is the time?

VEDIO

It is past nine.

PRINZIVALLE

Marco Colonna has not returned?

Monna Vanna

The sentries at the moat will bring him to
you the moment he arrives.

PRINZIVALLE

He had been here ere this were my offer
rejected . . . This hour decides; and it holds
all my life, like the great ships with flowing
sails that prisoners dream of, as they stare
into the darkness around them . . . It is
strange that a man should thus confide all his
destiny, his brain, his soul, his joy and his
sorrow, to a thing so frail as the love of a
woman! . . . I could smile at it myself, were
it not stronger than my smile . . . Marco
does not return . . . She will come, therefore . . . Go, look for the beacon which de-
clares her consent . . . See whether the light
be there that heralds the trembling footsteps
of the woman who gives herself that the
others may live, and saves me at the same
time as she saves her people . . . No, stay—
I will go myself. I have waited for this
hour since my boyhood, waited and yearned;
and no eyes but mine, not even those of a
friend, must be the first to greet its coming

190.

. . . [*He goes to the entrance of the tent,
flings back the curtain and looks into the
night.*] See, the light, Vedio, the light! See
how it shines and flares into the blackness!
. . . From the Campanile—that is well, that
is as it should be . . . See how it pierces the
gloom! . . . It is the only light that shines
on the town . . . Ah, never yet has Pisa
lifted to the skies so glorious a flower, waited
for so long and with so little hope! . . . Ah,
my brave Pisans! You shall hold festival
to-night that will linger long in your annals;
while I shall know a diviner joy than had I
saved my native city . . .

VEDIO

[*Touching his arm.*] Let us return to the
tent. Messer Trivulzio comes from yonder.

PRINZIVALLE

[*Coming back and dropping the curtain.*]
That is so. We must still . . . The interview will be brief . . . [*He goes to the table
and fingers the papers there.*] Have you his
three letters?

VEDIO

There are only two.

PRINZIVALLE

The two that I intercepted, and this evening's order . . .

VEDIO

Here are the first two. You are crumpling the other in your hand . . .

PRINZIVALLE

He is coming . . .

[*The guard raises the curtain. Enter* TRIVULZIO.]

TRIVULZIO

Have you observed the strange light that appears to be flashing signals from the Campanile? . . .

PRINZIVALLE

You think they are signals?

TRIVULZIO

I have no doubt of it . . . I must speak with you, Prinzivalle.

Monna Vanna

Say on. Leave us, Vedio, but do not go
far away; I shall want you. [VEDIO *goes.*]

TRIVULZIO

You are aware, Prinzivalle, of the high
esteem in which I hold you. This, indeed, I
have already proved to you more than once,
but there is much besides of which you are
ignorant; for the policy of Florence, which
people term perfidious, though it be merely
prudent, demands that many things should
be concealed even from those whom she ad-
mits to her most intimate secrets. We all
obey her profound orders; and each one of
us must courageously support the weight of
her mysteries, which are the emanation of her
supreme intelligence. Let it suffice, then,
that I tell you that I had a very good share
in your election, notwithstanding your youth
and unknown origin, to the command of the
most magnificent army the Republic has ever
put into the field; nor, indeed, has there ever
been cause to regret this choice. But for
some time now a party has been forming
against you. I am not sure whether, in re-

vealing this to you, I am not allowing the sincere friendship in which I hold you to infringe somewhat upon my duty. There are often occasions, however, when a too narrow clinging to duty may work more mischief than the very rashest generosity. Know, therefore, that you have enemies who accuse you most bitterly of indecision, vacillation, sloth. Others even go so far as to throw doubt upon your loyalty. Carefully framed slanders have been set on foot, which lend colour to these insinuations. They have produced a disastrous effect upon that section of the Assembly that already eyed you with disfavour. These have gone so far as to discuss your arrest, and your trial. Fortunately, I was advised in time. I hastened to Florence, and had no difficulty in opposing proof to proof. I stood surety for you. It remains for you now to justify my confidence, which has never for an instant wavered; for we are lost if you do not act. My colleague, Messer Maladura, is held in check at Bibbiena by the troops of the Venetian Proveditor. Another army is marching upon Florence from the North. The city is in danger.

194

All may yet be well if on the morrow you deliver the assault for which we have waited so
long. This will set free our finest army, as
well as the only captain whom victory has
never forsaken; and we shall be able to return
proudly to Florence, amidst the pomp and
triumph that shall turn your enemies of yesterday into your most fervent admirers and
partisans . . .

PRINZIVALLE

Is this all you have to say to me?

TRIVULZIO

Very nearly; though I have passed over in
silence the very real affection in which I hold
you, which has indeed grown with every day
of our intercourse. And this, notwithstanding the difficult position in which we are often
placed by laws that seem contradictory; laws
which demand that the authority of the general should at times—at moments of danger
—be balanced by the mysterious power of
Florence, whereof I am to-day the humble
representative . . .

PRINZIVALLE

This order that I have just received was written by you?

TRIVULZIO

Yes.

PRINZIVALLE

By your own hand?

TRIVULZIO

Undoubtedly.   Why this question?

PRINZIVALLE

These two letters—you recognise them?

TRIVULZIO

Perhaps.   I know not; what do they contain? . . . I must first . . .

PRINZIVALLE

There is no need.   I know.

TRIVULZIO

Are they the two letters you intercepted, as I hoped you might? . . . I see that the test was good.

Monna Vanna

You are not dealing with a child. Let us
not fall back on such wretched tricks as
these; or prolong an interview that I am
eager to end, that, indeed, delays a reward
which no triumph in Florence could ever
equal! . . . In these letters you have most
basely and falsely denounced every action of
mine. Was this from pure malice, or to pro-
vide the treacherous avarice of Florence with
the indispensable excuse for dealing cheaply
with a victorious mercenary? . . . In these
letters all things are distorted with so fiend-
ish a skill, that there are moments when I
doubt my own innocence. My every action
has been disfigured, degraded, besmirched;
and this from the very first week of the siege,
down to the hour when my eyes were opened—
the fortunate hour when I resolved to justify
your suspicions. I have had your letters
carefully copied—I have sent them to Florence. I intercepted the answer. Your word
is accepted, you are believed: the more readily
inasmuch as you had been supplied with the
theme of your accusation. I am judged, un-

heard; I am condemned to death . . . And
I know full well that not all the innocence of
the archangels could help me to escape from
the damning proofs that you have provided
. . . And therefore do I now spring forward,
burst your puny chains, and take the initia-
tive. Hitherto, I have been no traitor; but
since these two letters fell into my hands I
have been preparing your ruin. This night
I shall sell you, you and your sorry masters;
I shall deal you the cruellest, the most fatal
blow that lies in my power. And I shall regard it as the noblest deed of all my life, thus
to have humbled the one city that exalts
treachery to a virtue, and seeks to govern the
universe by means of fraud and hypocrisy,
lies, ingratitude, and villainy . . . For this
evening, thanks to me, Pisa, your ancient
enemy, who prevents you, and shall prevent
you, whilst her walls stand, from spreading
corruption over all the world—this evening
Pisa shall be saved, and shall lift her head to
breathe defiance once more . . . Ah, do not
rise, or make vain gestures . . . My measures have all been taken, and they are inevitable; you are in my power; and even as I

hold you now do I seem to hold in my hand
the destiny of Florence . . .

> [TRIVULZIO *draws his dagger and aims
> a swift blow at* PRINZIVALLE.]

TRIVULZIO

Not yet . . . Not while my hands are
free . . .

> [PRINZIVALLE, *warding off the blow
> with his arm, has thrown up the
> weapon, which strikes him in the
> face. He seizes* TRIVULZIO *by the
> wrist.*]

PRINZIVALLE

I was not prepared for this spasm of
terror . . . See, I hold you now, and can
crush you with one hand . . . I have only
to lower this dagger . . . It would seem already to be seeking your throat. What, you
say nothing? are you not afraid, then?

TRIVULZIO

[*Coldly.*] No; use the dagger, it is your
right. I knew my life was forfeit.

Monna Vanna

[*Loosening his hold.*] Ah . . . But, truly, then, this thing is strange that you have done . . . And even very rare . . . There are not many soldiers who would so readily clasp the hand of death; and I should not have thought that within so feeble a body . . .

TRIVULZIO

You men of the sword are only too apt to believe that there is no other courage than that which dwells at the end of a blade . . .

PRINZIVALLE

You may be right . . . It is well . . . You are not free, but no harm shall be done you . . . We serve different gods, you and I. [*He wipes the blood from his face.*] Ah, the blow was not unskilful . . . A little too hasty, but not lacking in vigour . . . It went within an ace of . . . And now, tell me, what would you do, if you held a man in your hands who had been so nigh despatching you to a world whither no one is anxious to go?

Monna Vanna

TRIVULZIO

I should not spare him.

PRINZIVALLE

I do not understand you . . . You are
strange . . . Confess that it was a despic-
able thing to write those letters. I have shed
my blood for Florence in three great battles;
I have never spared myself, I have strained
every nerve, the gain was all yours. I was
a faithful servant to the Republic, nor did
one single thought of disloyalty ever enter
my heart . . . You must have known this,
you who were always spying upon me . . .
And yet, in your letters, some vile malice or
hatred caused you to distort every action of
mine, every step that I took. I thought only
of Florence; you heaped slander on slander,
and lie upon lie . . .

TRIVULZIO

The facts were fallacious—that mattered
but little. It was for me to guard against
the dangerous hour when the soldier, flushed
by two or three victories, is on the point of
no longer obeying the master he serves, whose

mission is loftier than his. That hour had
sounded, as this hour proves. The people of
Florence held you too fondly. It is for us to
shatter their idols. They show some resent-
ment at the time, but they have created us
that we may oppose their dangerous caprices ;
and it seemed to me that the hour had come
to mark out their idol for destruction. I
warned Florence. She knew what my falsehoods meant . . .

PRINZIVALLE

The hour had not come, and would never
have come, but for your shameful letters . . .

TRIVULZIO

It might have come, and that was suffi-
cient . . .

PRINZIVALLE

What! Is an innocent man to be sacrificed
to a mere possibility? Offered up in cold
blood to a danger that never might threaten?

TRIVULZIO

What is the life of one man to the safety
of Florence!

Monna Vanna

PRINZIVALLE

You believe, then, in the destiny of Florence, in her work, her existence? She must be something, then, that I do not understand? . . .

TRIVULZIO

Yes, I believe only in her; the rest is nothing to me . . .

PRINZIVALLE

After all, it may be so . . . And you are right, since you believe . . . I have no country, I cannot tell. There are times when I regret that I have no country . . . But I have something that you never shall have— that no man ever has had as much as I . . . That atones for all . . . Go; let us part; we have no time to weigh these enigmas . . . We are far removed from each other, and yet there are points where we almost touch . . . Each man has his destiny . . . Some follow an idea, and others a desire; and it would be as hard for you to change your idea as for me to change my desire . . . Fare you well, Trivulzio; we go different ways . . . Give me your hand.

TRIVULZIO

Not yet.   I shall give you my hand on the
day of punishment . . .

PRINZIVALLE

Be it so; to-day you have lost; you will win
to-morrow . . . [*He calls* "VEDIO!"]

[VEDIO *comes in.*]

VEDIO

Master! . . . What, you are wounded, the
blood is flowing . . .

PRINZIVALLE

No matter . . . Summon the two guards.
Let them take this man away; but see that
they do him no injury. . . . He is an enemy
whom I love . . . Let them bestow him in
some safe place, where no one shall see him
. . . They answer for his safety, and shall
set him free at my command . . .

[VEDIO *goes, leading* TRIVULZIO.
PRINZIVALLE *stands before a mirror
and examines his wound.*]

PRINZIVALLE

The wound is not deep, but it has bitten

into my face . . . Who could have thought
that so feeble and haggard a man . . .
[VEDIO *returns.*] You have done as I bid
you?

VEDIO
Yes. Master, this will mean ruin . . .

PRINZIVALLE
Ruin! . . . Ah, that I could be ruined thus
each day to the day of my death! . . . Ruin,
Vedio! . . . Why, never yet in this world
will a legitimate revenge have brought to a
man a happiness like mine—a happiness of
which he has dreamed ever since he first
learnt to dream . . . I have waited and
prayed for it! I would have allowed no
crime to stop me, for it was mine, it belonged to me, and I was bound to have it;
and now that my star, urged on by justice,
by pity, sends it to me, upon its silvery rays,
you speak of ruin! . . . Oh, poor men with
cold hearts! . . . Poor men without love!
. . . Do you not know, then, that at this
moment my destiny is being balanced in the
sky, and that they are granting me the share
of a hundred lovers, the share of a thousand

joys! . . . Ah, I know it! . . . I touch the moment when those marked out for grand disaster or triumph suddenly find themselves on the topmost peak of their life, where all things belong to them and obey them, and become moulded to their hand! . . . And what matters the rest, and all that comes after! . . . There is an ecstasy too great for man, and it crushes him who achieves it! . . .

VEDIO

[*Approaching him with a linen bandage.*] The blood still flows; let me bind up your face.

PRINZIVALLE

Yes. Since it must be . . . But see that your bandages do not cover my eyes. [*Looking into the mirror.*] Ah, I seem more like a patient shrinking from a surgeon's knife than a lover who soon will be joyfully welcoming his love! . . . [*He shifts the bandage.*] And you, Vedio, my poor Vedio, what will become of you?

VEDIO

Master, where you go I go too . . .

Monna Vanna

PRINZIVALLE

Nay, you must leave me . . . I know not whither I shall go, nor what will become of me . . . Do you make good your escape; none will follow you, whereas if you go with your master . . . In these coffers is gold; take it, it is yours, I need it no longer . . . Are the waggons ready, the flocks all gathered?

VEDIO

They are in front of the tent.

PRINZIVALLE

Good. When I give the signal you will do what has to be done. [*The sound of a gunshot is heard from afar.*] What is that?

VEDIO

A shot has been fired at the outposts.

PRINZIVALLE

Who gave the order? . . . It must be a mistake . . . If they should have fired at her! Did you not tell . . .

VEDIO

Yes. It is impossible. I placed a number of guards there, who will bring her to you the moment that she arrives.

PRINZIVALLE

Go and see.   [*Exit* VEDIO.]

[For a moment PRINZIVALLE *remains alone.* VEDIO *returns, raises the curtain at the entrance, and murmurs " Master." Then he withdraws and* MONNA VANNA, *wrapped in a long mantle, appears, and pauses on the threshold.* PRINZIVALLE *trembles, and moves toward her.]*

VANNA

[In a stifled voice.] I have come as you bade me . . .

PRINZIVALLE

There is blood on your hand: are you wounded? . . .

VANNA

A ball touched my shoulder . . .

208

PRINZIVALLE

What? When? . . . This is terrible . . .

VANNA

As I drew near the camp.

PRINZIVALLE

Who fired the shot? . . .

VANNA

I know not; the man fled.

PRINZIVALLE

Are you in pain? . . .

VANNA

No.

PRINZIVALLE

Shall I have the wound dressed?

VANNA

No. It is nothing. [*A moment's silence.*]

PRINZIVALLE

Your mind is made up? . . .

Monna Vanna

VANNA

Yes.

PRINZIVALLE

Shall I remind you of the conditions?

VANNA

There is no need.

PRINZIVALLE

You have no regrets? . . .

VANNA

Was it stipulated that I should come without regrets?

PRINZIVALLE

Your husband consents? . . .

VANNA

Yes.

PRINZIVALLE

There still is time if you wish to renounce . . .

VANNA

No.

PRINZIVALLE

But why are you doing this?

Monna Vanna

VANNA

Because out yonder they perish of hunger, and to-morrow a still swifter death would await them . . .

PRINZIVALLE

There is no other reason?

VANNA

What other could there be? . . .

PRINZIVALLE

I can conceive that a virtuous woman . . .

VANNA

Yes.

PRINZIVALLE

One who loves her husband . . .

VANNA

Yes.

PRINZIVALLE

Deeply?

VANNA

Yes.

PRINZIVALLE

You are clad only in your mantle?

Monna Vanna

VANNA

Yes.

PRINZIVALLE

You have seen the chariots and flocks in front of the tent?

VANNA

Yes.

PRINZIVALLE

There are two hundred waggons filled with the best Tuscan wheat; two hundred others laden with forage, and with fruit and wine from Sienna. There are thirty more filled with German powder, and fifteen smaller ones laden with lead; and around them are six hundred oxen from Apulia, and twelve hundred sheep. They await your order to march into Pisa. Would you care to see them start?

VANNA

Yes.

PRINZIVALLE

Come then to the door of my tent.

> [*He raises the tapestry, gives the order, and makes a signal. A sound is heard as of a vague and mighty movement. Torches are*

*kindled and waved to and fro.
Whips are cracked and waggons
creak. There is the bleating of
sheep and the lowing of oxen.
VANNA and PRINZIVALLE, erect on
the threshold of the tent, watch for
a moment the enormous convoy as
it starts forth, with torches flaming
in the starry night.]*

PRINZIVALLE

From this night, thanks to you, Pisa will
cease to be hungry. She is invincible now,
and to-morrow will know the glory of a joy
and triumph for which none had dared any
longer to hope . . . Are you satisfied?

VANNA

Yes.

PRINZIVALLE

Let us close the tent then; and give me
your hand. The evening is still mild, but
the night will be cold. You have no weapons
concealed about you, no poison?

Monna Vanna

VANNA
I have only my sandals and this mantle.
Search me if you are afraid . . .

PRINZIVALLE
It is not for myself that I fear, but for
you . . .

VANNA
I place the life of my people high above
all . . .

PRINZIVALLE
It is well, and you have done right . . .
Come, sit here . . . It is a warrior's couch,
rugged and fierce, narrow as a tomb, and but
little worthy of you . . . Lie here, on these
tiger-skins, that have never yet felt the gentle
touch of a woman . . . Place this soft fur
at your feet . . . It is the skin of a lynx
that an African monarch gave me on the
night of a victory . . .

> [VANNA *sits, closely wrapped in her
> mantle.*]

PRINZIVALLE
The light of the lamp is falling on your
eyes; shall I move it?

Monna Vanna

VANNA

VANNA

It matters not . . .

PRINZIVALLE

[*Kneeling at the foot of the couch and seiz-ing* VANNA'S *hand.*] Giovanna! . . . [VANNA *starts up in surpise and looks at him.*] Oh, Vanna, my Vanna . . . for I, too, used to call you thus . . . Now I tremble as I speak your name . . . It has so long re-mained trebly sealed in my heart that it can-not escape without breaking its prison . . . Indeed, it is my heart, it is all I have . . . In each one of its syllables lies all my life, and as I pronounce them I feel my life flow from me . . . It was familiar to me; I thought I knew it; I had said it again and again to myself, until I ceased to be afraid: I had spoken it every hour of every day, like a great word of love that one yearns to utter, if it be only once, in the presence of her whom it has so long evoked in vain . . . I thought that my lips had shaped themselves to its form; that at the long-sought-for moment they would pronounce it so softly, so meekly, so humbly, with so profound and mighty a

215

yearning, that she who should hear it would
know the distress and the love that it held.
. . . Whereas to-day it is merely a shadow.
It is no longer the same . . . My fears
and sorrows have bruised it and crushed it,
and I can scarcely recognise it as it leaves
my lips. All the meaning and adoration
that I have placed within it come now
to break my strength and extinguish my
voice . . .

VANNA

Who are you?

PRINZIVALLE

You do not know me? . . . I recall no
memory? . . . Ah, the marvels that time
effaces! . . . But it is true that I alone had
seen those marvels . . . And it is better,
perhaps, that they should be forgotten . . .
I shall hope no longer, I shall have fewer regrets! . . . No, I am nothing to you . . .
A poor wretch, who for one single instant
wistfully gazes at what has been the aim of
his life; an unhappy man who asks nothing,
who knows not even what it is he should ask;
and yet he would, were it possible to him, tell

you before you go of what you have been to
him, and will be, to the very end of his
life . . .

VANNA

You know me then? . . . Who are
you? . . .

PRINZIVALLE

You do not remember the man who is looking at you now, as, in a fairy world, one
would look at the very source of one's joy
and existence? . . .

VANNA

No . . . At least I do not believe . . .

PRINZIVALLE

Yes, you have forgotten. . . . And I was
sure, alas, that you had forgotten! . . . You
were eight years old and I twelve when I met
you for the first time . . .

VANNA

Where? . . .

PRINZIVALLE

At Venice, one Sunday in June . . . My
father, the old goldsmith, brought your

217

mother a necklace of pearls. She was admiring the necklace—I strayed into the garden . . . I found you there, by the side of a pond, in a grove of myrtle . . . A slender golden ring had fallen into the water . . . You were crying on the bank . . . I sprang into the pond . . . The ring was glittering on the marble basin; I seized it and placed it on your finger . . . I was nearly drowned . . . But you kissed me and were happy . . .

VANNA

It was a fair-haired child named Gianello. Are you Gianello?

PRINZIVALLE

Yes.

VANNA

Who could have recognised you? . . . And besides, your face is covered with bandages . . . I can only see your eyes . . .

PRINZIVALLE

[*Shifting the bandages.*] Do you know me now that I move them?

Monna Vanna

VANNA

Yes, perhaps . . . I seem to . . . For
your smile is still that of a child . . . But
your are wounded, the blood is flowing . . .

PRINZIVALLE

Ah, it is not my first wound . . . But
that any one should have hurt you . . .

VANNA

Let me adjust your bandage, it is badly
tied. [*She winds the linen round his cheek.*]
I have often tended the wounded in this war
. . . Yes, yes, I remember . . . I can see
the garden again, with its pomegranates, its
roses and laurels. We played there more
than once, in the afternoon, when the sun
shone hot on the sand . . .

PRINZIVALLE

Twelve times in all—I kept count . . . I
can tell you each game that we played, and
every word that you said . . .

VANNA

Then, one day, I remember, I waited—for

I loved you well, you were so solemn, so quiet,
and treated me like a little queen . . . But
you never came back . . .

PRINZIVALLE

My father took me to Africa . . . There
we got lost in the desert . . . Then I was
taken prisoner by the Arabs, the Turks, the
Spaniards—that was my life. When I saw
Venice again your mother was dead; the
garden lay waste . . . I sought you in vain
. . . Till, at last, I heard of you, thanks to
your beauty, which no man could ever forget
who once had beheld it . . .

VANNA

You knew me at once when I came in?

PRINZIVALLE

Had ten thousand women come into my
tent, every one with a face like yours and
clad alike and equally beautiful, ten thousand
sisters whom their own kindred could not distinguish, I should have risen and taken you
by the hand and said, " This is she." . . . It
is strange, is it not, that an image one loves

should thus be able to dwell in the heart;
for in this heart of mine yours lived so profoundly that it grew and it changed . . . It
was different to-day from what it was yesterday; it blossomed, it became more beautiful; and the years adorned it with the gifts
they bring to the budding child . . . And
yet, when I saw you again it seemed at
first as though my eyes deceived me . . .
My memory, that had so faithfully treasured
your beauty, had yet been too timid, too halting; it had not dared to endow you with all
the glory which so suddenly flashed on my
sight. I was like a man who remembers a
flower he has only seen once as he crossed the
garden in twilight, and suddenly beholds a
hundred thousand flowers beneath the radiant
light of the sun . . . You came in, and I
saw the brow again that I knew so well, the
hair, and the eyes; I saw the soul in the face
I adored . . . But its beauty humbled the
one that I had been silently storing for days
and days, and months without end, and year
after year—the beauty that had fed on a
halting memory, and fallen so immeasurably
short of the real . . .

Monna Vanna

VANNA

Yes, you loved me as one loves at that age;
but time and absence throw a glamour over
love . . .

PRINZIVALLE

Men often say they have loved only once
in their life, but it rarely is true . . . To
disguise their indifference, or their desire,
they lay claim to the wonderful sorrow of
those who were born for a single love; and
when one of these tries to tell of the deep and
the dolorous truth that has furrowed his life,
the words that the fortunate lovers have used
so freely have lost all their strength, all their
gravity: and she who listens will uncon-
sciously degrade the poor sacred words, often
so full of sadness, to the trivial, playful
meaning they have for the majority of
men . . .

VANNA

I shall not do that. I can understand the
love for which we all yearn when our life
begins; the love we renounce because years—
although mine are few—put an end to many
things . . . But, tell me, when you passed

through Venice again and had found trace of me—tell me what happened then? You made no effort to see the woman whom you had loved so deeply? . . .

PRINZIVALLE

At Venice I learned that your mother was dead, that her fortune was lost, and that you were about to marry a great Tuscan noble, the richest and most powerful of all in Pisa, to whom you would be as a queen, adored and happy . . . I was an adventurer without a home, without a country—what was there that I could offer? . . . Destiny seemed to demand the sacrifice I grudgingly made to my love. Ah, how often have I wandered around the walls of this city, and clung to the chains of the gate, in my fear lest my longing to see you should overwhelm me, and disturb the love and the happiness that you had found . . . I hired out my sword, I engaged in two or three wars; I was a mercenary, and my name became known . . . I waited for the days to come, though hope had left me; till at last Florence despatched me to Pisa . . .

Monna Vanna

How feeble and cowardly men become when
they love! . . . Understand me well; I do not
love you, nor can I tell whether I could ever
have loved you . . . But it makes the very
soul of love leap and cry in my heart when I
find that a man who pretended to love as I
might myself have loved, had not more courage in the face of love . . .

PRINZIVALLE

It was not courage that failed me . . . I
had need of more than you think to be able to
go . . . But it was too late . . .

VANNA

It was not too late when you left Venice.
When one finds a love that fills a life, it never
can be too late . . . Such a love never renounces. Expecting nothing, it hopes. And
it persists, still, when it has ceased to hope.
Had I loved as you say you loved, then I
would have . . . Ah, one cannot say what
one would have done . . . But this much I
know: fate should not have wrenched my happiness from me without a struggle . . . I

224

should have cried to fate, "Hence, hence, I pass here!" . . . I should have forced the very stones to side with me! And whatever the cost, the man whom I loved should have learnt of my love, and himself have pronounced the sentence, and pronounced it more than once! . . .

PRINZIVALLE

[*Seeking her hand.*] You do not love him, Vanna?

VANNA

Whom?

PRINZIVALLE

Guido.

VANNA

[*Withdrawing her hand.*] Do not take my hand. I cannot give it to you. I see I must make myself clear. When Guido married me I was alone, almost poor; and the woman who is alone and poor soon falls victim to calumny, especially if her face be fair, and she scornful of artifice or falsehood . . . To these calumnies Guido paid no heed; he had faith in me, and his faith pleased me. He made me happy; at least as happy as one can be when one has renounced the vague and extravagant dreams which seem beyond human life; and I almost hope to convince you, too, that one can be happy without spending one's days in search of a happiness that no man ever has known. I love Guido to-day with a love less strange than the one you imagine you feel; but mine, at least, is steadier, calmer, more faithful, and more sure . . . That is the love that fortune has given me; I accepted it with my eyes open; I shall have no other; and if anyone breaks it that one will not be I . . . So you see you have misunderstood me. . . . When I tried to point out to you what I thought was an error of yours, it was not of you that I spoke, it was not of us: I spoke in the name of a love of which a glimpse descends on the heart at the very first dawn: a love which exists, perhaps, but that is not mine or yours; for you have not done what such a love would do . . .

PRINZIVALLE

You judge me harshly, Vanna, or rather this love of mine. You judge it with all too little knowledge of what it has done, and had

226

to suffer, in order to bring about this one happy moment that would most surely plunge every other love into despair . . . But though it had done nothing, and attempted nothing, I know of its existence, I who am its victim, whose life it has seized: I who bear it within me, and have lost all that makes for the joy and glory of man! . . . Ah, believe me, Vanna, and you must believe me, for I am of those who ask for nothing and hope for nothing! . . . You are in my tent now, and at my mercy . . . I have only to say a word, to stretch out my hand, and all is mine that the ordinary lover demands . . . But you know as well as I that the love of which I have spoken craves other things; therefore I ask that you no longer doubt me . . . I took your hand because I thought you would believe me . . . I shall not touch it again, my lips shall not press it; but, at least, Vanna, when we shall part to meet no more, at least know what kind of love mine has been, that it halted only before the impossible!

VANNA

From the moment that it could regard any-

thing as impossible, is not doubt permitted?
I demand no superhuman ordeals, no terrible
obstacles to be overcome. I ask for no proofs
of this kind, I am only too willing to believe
. . . Indeed, it is for the sake of your happiness, and mine, that I still would try to doubt
. . . In a love as mighty as yours there is
something sacred, that could not but disturb
the coldest of women . . . And therefore do
I probe into what you have done, and should
be almost happy could I discover nothing
that bears the stamp of this mortal passion,
on which fate so seldom smiles . . . And I
should have been convinced that I had found
nothing, but for this last act of yours; for
when I remember that you have madly
wrecked your future, your fame, all that you
have in the world, to bring me here for an
hour beneath this tent, then am I forced to
admit that possibly your love may be what
you say . . .

PRINZIVALLE

This last act is the only one that proves
nothing . . .

VANNA

How? . . .

Monna Vanna

PRINZIVALLE

I prefer that you should know the truth. In causing you to come to me here, in saving Pisa in your name, I have sacrificed nothing.

VANNA

I do not understand . . . Have you not betrayed your country, effaced your past services, ruined your future? What stands before you? Is it not exile or death?

PRINZIVALLE

In the first place I have no country. Otherwise, had my love been never so great, I should not have betrayed it for that love . . . But I am only a mercenary, faithful when others are faithful, a traitor when they betray . . . I have been falsely accused by the Florentine Commissioners, and condemned without trial by a Republic of merchants, whose ways you know as well as I. I was aware that I was lost; and the thing I have done to-night, far from hastening my ruin, will perhaps save me, if that still be possible . . .

Monna Vanna

So what you have sacrificed for my sake
counts but little?

It counts nothing at all . . . I could not
but tell you. I should have no joy in a smile
of yours that I had purchased with a lie . . .

Ah, Gianello, Gianello, this is worth more
than love and its noblest proofs! . . . You
need no longer seek the hand that fled from
you before. Take it . . .

I had rather that love had won it! . . .
But what matter, after all! . . . It belongs
to me, Vanna: I hold it between mine, I drink
its fragrance, I live its life, it is one with me
—I lose myself for a moment in the sweet
illusion . . . Ah, the dear hand! I open it,
close it, as though it could answer me in the
secret, mysterious language of lovers; I press
my kisses upon it, and you still let it lie here
. . . You forgive me, then, the cruel ordeal
to which I exposed you? . . .

VANNA

I should have done the same thing; better, perhaps, or worse, had I been in your place . . .

PRINZIVALLE

Did you know who I was when you agreed to come to my tent? . . .

VANNA

No one knew. There were strange rumours . . . According to some, Prinzivalle was a horrible old man; others declared him a young prince of marvellous beauty . . .

PRINZIVALLE

But Guido's father saw me; did he say nothing? . . .

VANNA

No.

PRINZIVALLE

You did not question him? . . .

VANNA

No.

PRINZIVALLE

But did your heart not fail you when you

came in the night, helpless, to the tent of an
unknown savage? . . .

VANNA

The sacrifice had to be made . . .

PRINZIVALLE

And when you saw me?

VANNA

At first the bandages hid your face . . .

PRINZIVALLE

Yes, but afterwards, Vanna, when I raised
them?

VANNA

Then it was different, and I already knew
you . . . But you, when you saw me enter
the tent—what was in your mind then; what
had you intended to do? . . .

PRINZIVALLE

Ah, how can I tell! . . . I knew I was lost,
I had the wild craving to drag all things
down with me . . . And I hated you because

232

of this love of mine! I marvel now at myself
when I think of it . . . There needed but a
word that was not yours, a gesture different
from your gestures, to unchain the brute
within me and fan my hatred . . . But the
moment I saw you I realised how impossible
it was . . .

VANNA

So did I realise it, too, and all fear left me,
for we understood each other without a word
being said. And it is all very strange . . .
I should have done this thing, too, I believe,
had I loved like you . . . Indeed, there are
moments, as I listen to you, when I fancy
that I am speaking, and that your words are
my words, and you hearing what I am saying . . .

PRINZIVALLE

I, too, Vanna, I felt at once that the wall
which divides us from all other beings was
growing transparent; it was as though I had
plunged my hands into a flowing stream, and
withdrawn them sparkling with light, shining with confidence and sincerity . . . And
it seemed to me that men were changed,

that all I had hitherto thought had been wrong . . . Most of all did I feel that I myself was changed, emerging at last as from a long imprisonment; that the gates were opening, flowers and leaves entwining around the bars; that the snows were melting on the far horizon, and the pure air of the morning entering my soul and breathing upon my love! . . .

VANNA .

In me, too, there was a change. I was surprised to find myself speaking to you as I did from the very beginning . . . I am habitually silent . . . I have never spoken thus to any man, save it be to Marco, Guido's father, and even with him it is different . . . He is wrapped in a thousand dreams; our conversations are rare . . . and, as for the others, there is always a look in their eyes that chills me. How dare I tell them I love them, or that I yearn to know what is passing in their heart? . . . Your eyes do not repel, they do not alarm . . . I felt at once that I knew you, though I could not recall where it was I had seen you before . . .

234

Monna Vanna

Could you have loved me, Vanna, had my evil star not brought me to you when it was too late? . . .

VANNA

Were I to tell you that I could have loved you, it would be the same as my telling you that I love you now, Gianello, and you know as well as I that cannot be . . . But we speak to each other here as though we were on a desert island . . . Were I alone in the world there would be no more to say . . . But we forget the suffering that another endures, while we two smile at the past . . . When I think of Guido's sorrow as I left Pisa, the despair in his eyes, his haggard face—oh, I can wait no longer! . . . Dawn must be close at hand, and I am so eager to know! . . . I hear a footstep, some one is passing the tent . . . People are whispering behind the curtain . . . Listen, listen! . . . What is it?

> [*The sound of whispers and hurried footsteps is heard outside the tent. Then the voice of* VEDIO *from without.*]

VEDIO

[*Off.*]   Master!

PRINZIVALLE

It is Vedio.   Come in!   Well?

VEDIO

[*At the entrance of the tent.*]   Quick,
quick!   Master, you must fly!   Lose not an
instant!   Messer Maladura, the second Commissioner of Florence . . .

PRINZIVALLE

He was at Bibbiena . . .

VEDIO

He has returned . . . Six hundred Florentines are with him . . . I saw them pass.
The camp is in uproar . . . He brings
orders . . . He proclaims you traitor . . .
He now seeks Trivulzio, and if he should find
him while you are still here . . .

PRINZIVALLE

Come, Vanna . . .

236

VANNA

Whither shall I go?

PRINZIVALLE

Vedio, with two men on whom I can rely, shall escort you to Pisa . . .

VANNA

And you, what will you do?

PRINZIVALLE

I know not, and it matters little. The world is wide enough—I shall find shelter.

VEDIO

Oh, master, beware! They hold the country all round the town, and Tuscany is full of spies . . .

VANNA

Come to Pisa.

PRINZIVALLE

With you? . . .

VANNA

Yes.

PRINZIVALLE

I cannot . . .

237

VANNA

If only for a few days . . . to put them
off the scent . . .

PRINZIVALLE

What will your husband do? . . .

VANNA

He will not fail in his duty to a
guest . . .

PRINZIVALLE

Will he believe you when you tell him? . . .

VANNA

Yes . . . —If he did not believe me . . .
But he will, he must . . . —Come . . .

PRINZIVALLE

No.

VANNA

Why?—What do you fear?

PRINZIVALLE

It is for you that I fear . . .

VANNA

For me? For me the danger is the same

whether I be alone or with you. It is for you we must fear, for you who have saved Pisa; now it is right that Pisa should save you . . . You come under my protection, and I stand surety for you . . .

PRINZIVALLE

So be it: I will go with you . . .

VANNA

You could give me no better proof of your love . . . Come. Let us lose no time . . . Throw open the tent . . .

[PRINZIVALLE, *followed by* VANNA, *moves to the entrance and throws the tapestry wide open. There is a vast murmur of voices and clashing of arms; but above all is heard the sound of distant bells, pealing joyfully, that burst sharply upon the silence of the night. Far away in the distance Pisa is seen on the horizon, brilliantly illuminated. Great bonfires throw a mighty glare on the dark sky.*]

Monna Vanna

Look, Vanna, look!

What is it, Gianello? . . . Oh, I understand! . . . These are the fires of joy that they have kindled, to celebrate what you have done . . . The walls are aglow, the ramparts glitter, the Campanile shines like a torch of gladness. See how the radiant towers are whispering to the stars! . . . And the very streets are reflected in the sky: I can recognise the road I trod this evening! . . . There is the piazza with its dome of fire; and the Camp Santo, that makes an island of shadows! . . . One could almost imagine that life, but now at its very last gasp, had rushed back to Pisa, leaping from spire to spire, flinging itself across the skies, flooding the walls, the whole country, and now making signals to us, and calling us back . . . Listen, listen! . . . Hark to the shouts, the ecstasy, the delirium, rising and swelling, as though the sea were invading Pisa! . . . Hark to the bells, the bells that sound as they did at my wedding . . . Ah, I am happy,

happy, and happiest of all to owe my happiness to you, to you who have loved me best! . . . Come, my Gianello! [*She kisses him on the brow.*] That is the only kiss I can give you . . .

PRINZIVALLE

Oh, my Giovanna, it is the most exquisite kiss that love could hope for! . . . But see, you tremble; your knees bend under you! . . . Come, lean on me, put your arm round me . . .

VANNA

It is nothing: I am faint—I have over-taxed my strength. Help me, carry me! Let nothing hinder my first happy steps . . . How beautiful is the night beneath the wakening dawn! . . . Quick! Let us hasten, it is time. We must arrive before the joy has faded . . .

[*They go out together,* PRINZIVALLE *supporting* VANNA.]

ACT III

State Apartment of GUIDO COLONNA

(Lofty windows, porticos, marble columns, &c. To the left, at back, a terrace, the approach to which is by a great double staircase. On the balustrade of the terrace are huge vases filled with flowers. In the centre of the room, between the columns, ample marble steps lead to the terrace, which commands a view over a great part of the town. Enter MARCO, GUIDO, BORSO, *and* TORELLO.)

GUIDO

I YIELDED to you, to her, to every one; but now it is only just that I should have my turn. I have been silent, I have held my breath, I have hidden—as a coward might hide while thieves are plundering his house.

But, in my degradation, I have still retained my honour . . . You have made a tradesman of me, a huckster, a weaver of cunning bargains . . . But now the dawn has come . . . I have not budged from my place . . . A contract was made, I had to respect it: I had to purchase your food . . . This night, this noble night, belonged to the buyer . . . Ah, who knows, it was not too high a price, perhaps, to pay for this wheat, for all these sheep and oxen . . . Now you have eaten your fill, and I have paid . . . Now I am free, I am master once more; and I hurl my shame from me! . . .

MARCO

My son, I know not what your intentions may be, and no one has the right to intrude upon a grief like yours . . . Words cannot soften it, and I can well understand that the happiness which it has caused, which surrounds you on every side, can only embitter it, and render it more poignant . . . The city is saved, but we almost regret the salvation which has cost you so dear; and we bend our heads before you who have had to bear the whole burden . . . And yet, could we recall yesterday, I should still have to act as I did, mark out the same victims, and plead for the same injustice; for the man who would be just is compelled all his life sorrowfully to choose between two or three acts of varying injustice . . . I know not what to say to you; but if this voice of mine that once you loved could for the last time reach your heart, I would beg of you, my son, not blindly to follow the first counsels of anger and grief . . . Wait, at least, until the dangerous hour be past which impels us to utter words that cannot be recalled . . . Vanna will soon be here. Do not judge her to-day. Do nothing irrevocable . . . For all that one does and says beneath the empire of an overpowering grief is so naturally, so cruelly, irrevocable! . . . Vanna will return, rejoicing, despairing . . . Do not reproach her . . . If you do not feel yourself strong enough to speak to her as you will speak after many days, let some time pass before you see her . . . For in us poor creatures, who are merely the playthings of irresistible forces, there resides so much goodness, and justice,

and wisdom, in the years that pass; and the
only words that count, that we must eagerly
grope for when misfortune blinds us, are
those that we shall pronounce when full un-
derstanding has come, when we have forgiven
and once more begun to love . . .

GUIDO

You have finished? It is well. This is no
longer the hour for honeyed phrases, nor is
there any one here to-day whom they still can
deceive . . . I have suffered you, and for
the last time, to say what you had to say; for
I was curious to know what your wisdom
could offer me in exchange for the life it has
so effectually ruined . . . See what it gives
me! To wait, to be patient, to accept, forget, to pardon and weep! . . . Well, no!
That does not suffice! . . . I had rather not
be wise, and get rid of my shame! Words
cannot do this for me . . . And as for my
intentions, they are very simple—I shall act
as you would have urged me to act but a
few years ago. A man has taken Vanna
from me; Vanna is no longer mine while this
man exists. For I, you see, am guided by

other rules than those that govern the verb
and the adjective. I obey the great law before which every man bends whose heart is
alive within him . . . Pisa has food now,
weapons; she can eat, she can fight; very
well, I claim my share. From this day on-
wards her fighting men are mine, or, at least,
the best of them—those I myself recruited
and paid for, out of my purse. I have dis-
charged my duty to Pisa—now I demand my
own. These men shall not go back to her until they have done what I in my turn have
now the right to exact . . . As for the rest
—for Vanna—I forgive her, or shall forgive
her when this man has ceased to be . . . She
has been deceived, she has been led astray;
but, at least, there was heroism in what she
did . . . The foulest advantage was taken
of her mercy, her greatness of soul . . . Be
it so . . . To forget may be impossible; but
at least this deed of hers may fade so remotely
into the past that it shall hide itself from
the love that seeks it . . . But there exists
one creature whom I shall never behold without shame and horror . . . A man is here
whose sole mission in life was to be the guide,

the prop, of a great and noble happiness. He
has become its enemy, and its scourge; and
there shall happen before you all a thing that
is terrible and yet is just . . . You shall
see a son, who, in a world for a moment out
of gear, judges his own father, denies him,
and curses him; thrusts him from his presence, despises and hates him! . . .

MARCO

Curse me, my son, but pardon her . . . If
there be in this heroic act that has saved so
many lives a fault that cannot be pardoned,
then is that fault all mine, but the heroism
hers . . . My advice was good; but advice
was easy for me, who bore no share in the
sacrifice; and to-day, when it deprives me of
all that I hold dearest in the world, it seems
still better to me than it did before . . . I
have no right to quarrel with your judgment;
when I was younger I should have judged like
you . . . I go, my son, and you shall behold
me no more; I can well understand that my
presence is odious to you—and yet I shall try
to see you again without being seen by you
. . . And since I depart, scarce daring to

hope that I may live to see the hour when you
will pardon the wrong I have done you—for
my own past reminds me that pardon comes
slowly when one is still in the prime of life—
since I leave you thus, let me, at least, be
convinced that I take with me all your hatred
and bitterness, all your cruel memories; and
that none will remain for her who is to come
. . . Beyond this I have but one prayer . . .
Let me, and for the last time, see her throw
herself into your arms . . . Then I shall go
without a murmur, without deeming you unjust . . . It is good that in human sorrow
the oldest should take on his shoulders all
that he can bear; seeing that he has but few
steps before him ere his burden shall fall
aside . . .

> [*Already during* MARCO's *last words,
a vague and mighty murmur has
been heard from without. In the
silence that follows, this noise increases, drawing nearer and becoming more and more distinct. First
there is an expectant stir, then still
distant shouts of a crowd rushing
from point to point. Soon the*

*vague cries take form, and one
hears from all sides, more and more
clearly, repeated a thousand times,
" Vanna, Vanna, our Monna Vanna!
Glory to Monna Vanna, Vanna,
Vanna, Vanna! "*]

MARCO

[*Rushing to the porticos that open on to
the terrace.*] It is Vanna! . . . She returns!
. . . She is there! . . . They acclaim her;
they acclaim her! Listen, listen!

[BORSO *and* TORELLO *follow him to
the terrace, while* GUIDO *remains
alone, leaning against a pillar and
looking straight before him. All
this time the noise from without becomes louder and draws rapidly
nearer.*]

MARCO

[*On the terrace.*] Ah, see! The square,
the streets, the windows, the trees, are all
black with waving heads and arms! The
roofs, the tiles, the leaves, would seem to be
changed into men! . . . But where is Vanna?

249

I see only a cloud that shuts and opens . . .
Borso, my poor eyes play me false and betray
my love . . . Old age and tears are blinding
them . . . They cannot see the one creature
they yearn for . . . Where is she, where is
she? . . . Which way must I go to meet
her? . . .

BORSO

[*Holding him back.*] No; do not go down;
the people are wild, they have lost all control.
They are mad with excitement; women are
fainting, men trodden under foot! . . . Besides, it is useless; she comes, there she is,
there she is! . . . See, she raises her head!
. . . She sees us! . . . She is hurrying to
us! Ah, she looks up and smiles! . . .

MARCO

You see her, but I cannot! . . . These
moribund eyes of mine can distinguish nothing! . . . For the first time I curse the old
age that has taught me so much, and now
hides this one thing from me! . . . But you
who can see her, tell me how does she look?
. . . Can you see her face?

Monna Vanna

BORSO

She returns in triumph . . . She seems to shine on the people . . .

TORELLO

But who is the man who is walking by her side?

BORSO

I know not . . . I never have seen him; he hides his face . . .

MARCO

Hark, how they shout! . . . The whole palace trembles; the flowers fall from the vases on to the steps . . . The very flag-stones seem to be rising beneath us to sweep us along in this overpowering gladness . . . Ah, I begin to see . . . They are close to the gates! The crowd divides . . .

BORSO

Yes, before Vanna. They are making a lane for her, a lane of triumph, of love . . . In her path they throw flowers, palm leaves, jewels . . . . Mothers hold out their chil- dren for her to touch; men stoop to kiss the

251

stones her feet have trodden . . . Be careful,
they are too near us. They are mad with
joy . . . If they reach these steps we shall
all be swept away . . . Ah, it is well! The
guards are rushing from the other side to
bar the entrance! . . . I will give orders to
shut out the people and close the gates, if
there be yet time . . .

MARCO

No, no! Let joy blossom here as it blossoms in the people's hearts! It is their vast
love that speaks—let it do what it will! They
have suffered enough! . . . Now that salvation has come let no barrier hold them back!
Ah, my poor brave people, I, too, am drunk
with joy; I raise my voice with yours! . . .
Ah, Vanna, my Vanna! Is it you whom I
see on the steps? . . . [*He rushes forward
to meet* VANNA, *but* BORSO *and* TORELLO
hold him back.] Come, Vanna, come! They
are keeping me back! They are alarmed
at this mighty joy! Come, Vanna, come!
More beautiful than Judith, and purer than
Lucrece! . . . Come! . . . Here, in the
midst of the flowers! [*He runs to the marble*

*vases and seizes handfuls of flowers that he
hurls to the foot of the stairs.*]   I, too, have
flowers with which to greet the light!   I, too,
have lilies, laurels, and roses with which to
crown glory!

> [*The clamour becomes more and more
> delirious.* VANNA, *accompanied by*
> PRINZIVALLE, *appears on the top of
> the steps and throws herself into*
> MARCO's *arms. The crowd invade
> the palace stairs and the terrace;
> but, nevertheless, remain at a cer-
> tain   distance   from   the   group
> formed by* VANNA, PRINZIVALLE,
> MARCO, BORSO, *and* TORELLO.]

VANNA

My father, I am happy . . .

MARCO

[*Holding her close to him.*]   And I, too,
my child, since I behold you again! . . . Let
me look at you through my tears . . . I see
you more radiant than had you descended
from the depths of the sky, that now acclaims
your return! . . . The horrible foe has not

been able to rob your eyes of their light,
nor a single smile from your lips! . . .

VANNA

Father, I will tell you . . . But where is
Guido? . . . He must be the first to hear—
to be comforted, for how can he know?

MARCO

Vanna, Vanna, he is there . . . Come
. . . Me he repels, and justly, perhaps, but
there is forgiveness for you, for your glorious fault; and I yearn to see you sink into
his arms, that my last glance may fall upon
your love . . .

> [GUIDO *steps forward to* VANNA. *She
> is about to speak—to throw herself
> into his arms—but* GUIDO, *with a
> brusque movement, stops and repels
> her, and addresses himself to those
> round about him.*]

GUIDO

[*In a strident and imperious voice.*]   Go,
all! . . .

VANNA

No, no! They must wait! . . . Guido, I must tell you; I must tell them all . . . Guido, listen!

GUIDO

[*Stopping her and pushing her back, raising his voice in growing anger.*] Do not come near me, do not touch me! [*He advances towards the crowd, which has invaded the hall, but now recoils before him.*] Have you not heard me? I bade you go! Leave us! You are the masters in your own homes, but here I rule! Borso, Torello, summon the guard! Ah! I see what it means! You have had your food, and now you would feast your eyes on this merry spectacle! . . . No, no, you have meat and wine; I have paid for you all; is that not enough? Go, I tell you! [*Silent movement in the crowd, which slowly disperses.*] Let none venture to linger! [*He seizes his father violently by the arm.*] You, too! You, above all! You more than the others, since the fault is yours! You shall not see my tears! I desire to be alone. Lonelier than the tomb, to know what I have to know! [*Seeing* PRINZIVALLE, *who has not*

255

stirred.] And you? . . . Who are you who stand there like a veiled statue? . . . Are you death, or shame? Have you not understood that I told you to go? [*He snatches a halberd from a guard.*] Must I drive you hence with this halberd? . . . You touch your sword? . . . I, too, have a sword, but have other uses for it . . . Henceforth it serves against one man, and one man alone. . . . What veils are those that hide your head? . . . I am in no mood for a masquerade . . . You make no answer . . . I ask who you are? . . . Wait——

> [*He approaches and is about to tear away the bandages.* VANNA *rushes between and stops him.*]

VANNA

Do not touch him! . . .

GUIDO

[*In amazement.*] Vanna, what, Vanna? Whence comes this sudden strength?

VANNA

It is he who saved me . . .

256

GUIDO

Hah! He saved you . . . When it was too late . . . A noble action, truly . . . It would have been better . . .

VANNA

[*Feverishly.*] But let me tell you, Guido, I implore you! One word, but one word! . . . He saved me, he spared me, respected me! . . . He comes here with me, under my protection . . . I have given my word, your word, ours! . . . You are angry now, but listen to me; only listen! . . .

GUIDO

Who is this man?

VANNA

Prinzivalle . . .

GUIDO

Who? . . . . What? . . . He, that man? That man Prinzivalle!

VANNA

Yes, yes! He is your guest! He puts

257

himself into your hands! It is he who has saved me, Guido . . .

GUIDO

[*After a moment's stupor, with growing exultation and vehemence that render it impossible for* VANNA *to interrupt him.*] Ah, this, my Vanna! . . . Ah, this falls on my soul like dew from the innermost heaven! . . . Ah, Vanna, my Vanna! . . . Yes, you are right; since it had to be done, that was the way to do it! Ah, I understand your stratagem now! Yes, I see it all! . . . But I did not know, I could not imagine! . . . There are women who would have killed him, as Judith killed Holophernes! . . . But his crime is greater than that of Holophernes, and calls for a greater vengeance! . . . Therefore you brought him here; therefore you have led him into the midst of his victims, who now shall become his executioners! . . . Ah, the magnificent triumph! . . . He followed you meekly, tenderly; and did not suspect that the kisses you gave him were kisses of hatred! . . . Here he is, caught in a trap! . . . Yes, you were right! To have killed

258

him down there, alone in his tent, after his
horrible crime—that would not have sufficed!
. . . A doubt would have remained, we should
not have seen him . . . All had known of the
abominable compact; it was needful, therefore, that all should know the price to be
paid for such treachery! . . . But how did
you do it? . . . It is the greatest triumph
that ever a woman . . . Ah, you shall tell
them! [*He rushes to the terrace and shouts
at the top of his voice.*] Prinzivalle! Prinzivalle! The enemy is here! We hold him!

VANNA

[*Clinging to him and trying to keep him
back.*] No, no! Listen! Listen, Guido, I
implore you! Guido, Guido, you are wrong!

GUIDO

[*Shaking himself free, and shouting still
louder.*] Let me go! You shall see! They
must all of them know, all! [*Shouting to
the crowd.*] Come back, all of you! You
may, you must! . . . And you, too, my
father! You who are crouching there behind
the pillars, as though expecting a god to

spring forth to repair the wrong you caused,
and restore me my happiness! Come back!
This is joy, joy! There has been a great
miracle! I want the very stones to hear what
has happened! I need skulk in corners no
longer—that is all over—I shall go hence
purer than the purest, richer than those who
have lost nothing! Ah, now you can acclaim
my Vanna! I acclaim her with you, and
louder than you all!

[*The people hasten on to the terrace,
he drags them into the hall.*]

GUIDO

This time you shall see a spectacle! There
is a justice, after all! . . . Ah, I knew it
well, but could not believe that it could act so
promptly! . . . I thought years and years
must pass; that I should have to spend my
life seeking my foe, in towns, in forests, in
mountains! And, see, suddenly he springs up
before me here, in this very room, on these
steps, in front of us! An overpowering
miracle! . . . But we shall hear . . . It is
Vanna has done this! . . . And there shall be

justice! [*To* MARCO, *whom he seizes by the arm.*] You see that man? . . .

MARCO

Yes; who is he?

GUIDO

You have seen him before . . . You have spoken to him . . . You were his complaisant messenger . . .

> [PRINZIVALLE *turns his face to* MARCO, *who recognises him.*]

MARCO

Prinzivalle!   [*Movement in the crowd.*]

GUIDO

Yes, yes, it is he; there is not the least doubt . . . Come nearer. Look at him, touch him! He may have some new message to send, perhaps . . . Ah, he is no longer the magnificent Prinzivalle! But for him there shall be no pity . . . He took, by a vile and monstrous artifice, the one thing in the world that I could not give; and now he he has come to me. He has been brought hither by justice, by a stratagem more marvellous than justice, to ask of me the one recompense I can afford . . . Am I not right to call it a miracle? Come nearer, nearer! Have no fear; he cannot escape! And yet, see that the doors are shut; we must not allow another miracle to snatch him from us . . . We shall not deal with him at once . . . There shall be prolonged pleasures in store for him . . . Ah, you, my brothers, to whom he caused so much suffering; you whom he sought to massacre, whose wives and children he sold into slavery, look at him now! Yes, this is he; and he is mine, he is yours, he is ours, I tell you! . . . He has made you suffer, but what has your suffering been compared with mine? . . . He shall be yours, very soon . . . My Vanna has led him to us, that our vengeance may blot out our shame! . . . [*Addressing the crowd.*] Stand witness, all of you! There must not be one shadow of doubt . . . Have you thoroughly realised what a miracle of heroism this is? . . . That man took Vanna from me . . . I was helpless, I could do nothing: you sold her . . . I have curses for none . . . The past is past . . . You had the right to prefer your life to my poor happiness . . . But Vanna, my Vanna, has known how to build love anew with the thing that had killed it . . . You destroyed; she has recreated . . . Vanna has done it! . . . She is greater than Lucrece or Judith, Lucrece who killed herself, and Judith who slew Holophernes! Ah, that, truly, would have been too mild, too simple, too silent! . . . Vanna does not slay in a closed tent: she brings the victim to us, alive, and offers him to us all! . . . And how has she done this? . . . Listen, she will tell! . . .

VANNA

Yes, I will tell you; but it is all quite different . . .

GUIDO

[*Stopping her and throwing his arms round her.*] Let me kiss you first, before them all . . .

VANNA

[*Thrusting him violently back.*] No, no! Not yet! . . . No, no, never again if you will not hear me! Listen, Guido! I speak of

an honour more real, of a happiness greater
than those that are blinding you! Ah, I am
glad they have all returned! They will hear
me, perhaps, before you will: they will understand before you understand! Listen,
Guido! . . . You shall not touch me until
you know . . .

GUIDO

[*Interrupting her, and again trying to embrace her.*] Yes, yes, I know—but first of
all I will . . .

VANNA

Listen, I tell you! In all my life I have
never lied, but to-day I am telling the pro-
foundest truth, the truth one speaks only
once, that brings life or death in its train
. . . Listen; and look at me well; look at me
as though you had never seen me before this
hour, which is the first, the only one when you
truly can love me as I wish to be loved . . .
I speak to you now in the name of the life
we have lived together; in the name of all
that I am, of all that you are to me! . . .
Be capable of believing what, perhaps, can

264

be scarcely believed . . . I was in this man's power . . . I had been handed over to him: he did not come near me, he did not touch me . . . I come from his tent as from the home of a brother . . .

GUIDO

Why?

VANNA

Because he loves me . . .

GUIDO

Ah! so that was what you had to say to us! That was the miracle? . . . Yes, yes, at your very first words I saw there was something strange . . . It was only a flash, and I paid no heed . . . I thought that the trouble, the horror had . . . But I see now that we must look into it . . . So he did not come near you, you say; he did not touch you? . . .

VANNA

No.

GUIDO

Not even kiss you?

Monna Vanna

VANNA

I gave him one kiss on the brow, which he returned.

GUIDO

And you can tell this to me! . . . Vanna, Vanna, has this fearful night driven you mad?

VANNA

I tell you the truth.

GUIDO

The truth! Great God! it is that, and that alone, that I seek! But the truth must be human . . . What! a man who betrays his country, ruins his life, sets all the world against him for ever—and does all this that you should go to his tent alone—this man demands but a kiss on the brow; and comes to us here with you to make us believe it? . . . No, no; we must be just, and not gibe too much at misfortune . . . If this was all that he asked, why inflict so much misery upon our whole people? And flood me with such despair? . . . This night has lasted ten years: I have scarcely survived it! . . . Ah, had this been all he sought he could have

266

saved us without this torture! . . . We should have welcomed him like a god, like a deliverer! You shake your head . . . See, the people shall judge, the people shall answer. [*Addressing the crowd.*] Have you heard? I know not why she has said these things; but what she has said is said, and you shall be judges . . . You will believe her, perhaps, since she has saved you . . . If you believe her, speak . . . Let those who believe her step out from the crowd! . . . Let them come to us here, and give the lie to poor human reason! . . . Let them come, all those who believe! . . . I am anxious to look at them, and see what sort of men they are! . . .

> [MARCO *alone stands forth from the crowd. One hears only faint, dim, and indistinct murmurs.*]

MARCO

[*Rushing forward.*] I believe her!

GUIDO

You! You are their accomplice . . . But the others, the others, where are the rest

who believe? . . . [*To* VANNA.] Have you
heard? The people you saved shrink from
the laughter that would burst from every
corner of the hall . . . The few who murmured have not dared to show themselves,
and I——

VANNA

They have no cause to believe me; but you,
you who loved me!

GUIDO

Ah, I who loved you should therefore become your dupe! No, no! Now listen to
me! I speak to you calmly, I have ceased to
be angry . . . I have gone through too
much, I begin suddenly to feel old . . . No,
I am not angry . . . There is no anger left
in me—something else will take its place, I
suppose—old age, madness, I know not yet
. . . At present I look, I search, I grope in
myself, to discover the happiness that once
was mine . . . I have one hope, one hope
alone; a hope so frail that I scarcely can
grasp it . . . A word would destroy it; and
yet, in my despair, I must make the attempt
. . . Vanna, I was wrong to call back the
crowd before knowing . . . I should have

remembered how galling it must be to you to proclaim to them all that that monster had caused you to suffer . . . Yes, I should have waited until we were alone; then you would have confessed the truth, the horrible truth. But I know it, alas! and the others all know. Of what avail to hide it, Vanna? . . . It is too late . . . There is no help for it now; and you, too, must understand . . . In moments like these reason is incapable of——

VANNA

Look at me, Guido; all my loyalty, all my strength and my truth are in my eyes now as I speak! . . . The truth, the truth, believe it! . . . He did not touch me.

GUIDO

Good! It is good. It is very good! Now I know all, and all is gone from me . . . Yes, it is the truth; or rather, it is love. Ah, I understand; you seek to save him. I did not realise that the woman I loved could change so quickly. But not that way can he be saved! [*He raises his voice.*] Hear

me, all of you! I will for the last time swear
an oath . . . To restrain myself now demands superhuman effort; my hold on myself
is weakening. I make one final effort, there
is one moment yet before I break down . . .
That moment I will not lose . . . Can you
hear me, you all; or is my voice grown too
weak? Come nearer, nearer! . . . You see
this woman, that man; they love each other
. . . Well. Now hear me. I am weighing
all my words as scrupulously as one weighs
the medicine given to the dying . . . These
two shall go from me here, with my consent,
shall go freely, unmolested, untouched, un-
harmed. They shall take with them whatever they choose. You shall open your ranks
to afford them passage. You shall strew
their path with flowers, if it so please you.
They shall go wheresoever their love may
guide their footsteps; and all I ask in exchange is that this woman shall first of all
tell me the truth, the only possible truth
. . . That is the one thing left to me now
that I can still love in her . . . I demand
the truth that she owes me, in exchange for
what I will give her . . . You understand,

Vanna? you have only one word to say . . .
All here are witness . . .

VANNA

I have told you the truth . . . He did
not touch me . . .

GUIDO

It is well. You have spoken—you have
condemned him. Now there is nothing more
to be done. [*He calls the guards and
points to* PRINZIVALLE.] That man belongs
to me; take him and bind him; thrust him
into the lowest dungeon beneath this hall. I
shall go with you. [*To* VANNA.] You will
never see him again; but on my return I
shall report to you his last words . . .

VANNA

[*Throwing herself in the midst of the
guards, who are seizing* PRINZIVALLE *and
leading him away.*] No, no! I have lied, I
have lied. [*To* GUIDO.] Yes, what you say
is true! [*Pushing the guards away.*] Go,
you must not take what is mine! For he is
mine, he belongs to me, not to you! To me

271

alone! It is for me to punish—the coward who when I was helpless, defenceless . . .

PRINZIVALLE

[*Trying to drown her voice.*] She lies! She lies! She lies to save me, but torture me as you will——

VANNA

Be silent! [*Turning to the crowd.*] He is afraid! [*Approaching* PRINZIVALLE, *as though enforcing silence upon* PRINZIVALLE.] Give me chains, and irons! Now that I dare speak out my hatred, it is I who shall bind him, I who brought him here. [*Whispering to* PRINZIVALLE *as she ties his hands.*] Be silent! He saves us, be silent! He has joined us. I belong to you, I love you! I love you, my Gianello! I put these chains on you, but I shall guard you, and free you! We two shall fly together! [*Shouting as though enforcing silence upon* PRINZIVALLE.] Be silent! [*Addressing the crowd.*] He pleads for mercy! [*Uncovering his face.*] Look at his face; it was my dagger, my dagger inflicted that wound! Look at him!

He, the coward, the monster! [*Seeing that the guards make a movement as though to remove* PRINZIVALLE.] No, no, leave him to me! He is my victim, my prey! It is I who have bought him! He belongs to me!

GUIDO

Why did he come, and why did you lie to me?

VANNA

[*Hesitating and picking her words.*] Why I lied . . . I scarcely know, I did not want to say . . . Ah, well, I must tell you now . . . There are times when one scarcely knows what one does, and is groping in the dark . . . Yes, you shall know, you shall know, for now I have torn away the veil . . . It was the thought of your love, of your despair, that alarmed me . . . But I will tell you. [*In a calmer voice and with more assurance.*] No, no, I had not the idea you speak of . . . I did not bring him here that we two, you and I, should be publicly avenged in the midst of a crowd; my idea, perhaps, was less noble, but my love for you prompted me . . . I yearned to inflict a cruel death

273

upon him, but was anxious also that the
horrible memory of this horrible night should
not weigh upon you to the end of your days
. . . It was my intention to revenge myself
in the dark . . . To inflict a slow, lingering
death upon him . . . Do you see? . . . Kill
him slowly, little by little, till his blood, falling drop by drop, should have wiped out his
crime . . . You would never have known the
awful truth, and there would have been no
spectre between us . . . I feared, I confess,
that the memory of this would lessen your
love for me . . . I was foolish, I know . . .
It was mad to expect you to believe . . .
But now you shall learn all . . . [*Addressing the crowd*.] Hear me, and you shall
judge me! What I said before I said for
Guido's sake, for the sake of our love . . .
Now I shall tell you all . . . I tried to kill
that man; I wounded him, as you see . . .
But he disarmed me . . . Then I thought
of a deeper revenge, and I smiled on him; and
he, the fool, had faith in my smile . . . And
now he is here in his tomb, that I myself shall
seal down . . . I kissed him, and he believed
in my kiss; and he followed me, like a lamb

And I hold him now in my hands, and my
hands shall close down on him! . . .

GUIDO

[*Approaching.*] Vanna! . . .

VANNA

Look at me well! . . . So mad is this man,
he believed me at once when I said " Prinzivalle, I love you!" . . . Ah, he would have
followed me down to the heart of hell! . . .
And now he is my man; he is mine, before
God and the world! I have won, I have
bought him! . . . [*She totters and supports
herself against the column.*] Take care, I
fall. There is too much joy now, in the
thought of the vengeance to come! [*To*
MARCO.] Father, I entrust him to your
care, till I am stronger . . . You shall take
charge of him, find a prison for him, a profound dungeon into which no one shall enter
. . . And give me the key; I must have the
key; I want it at once No one shall touch
him, go near him; he belongs to me, to me;
he is mine; I alone shall punish . . . Guido,
he belongs to me! [*Stepping towards*

MARCO.] Father, he is mine; you shall answer for him. [*She looks fixedly at him.*]
You understand, you are his guardian. You
are responsible for him; not a hand shall approach him, and when I go to him he shall be
as he is, now that I give him to you. [PRIN-
ZIVALLE *is taken away.*] Fare you well, my
Prinzivalle! Ah, we shall meet again!

> [*While* GUIDO *is in the midst of
> the soldiers, who brutally remove*
> PRINZIVALLE, VANNA *screams, tot-
> ters, and falls into the arms of*
> MARCO, *who rushes forward to sup-
> port her.*]

MARCO

[*Rapidly, in a low voice, bending over*
VANNA *as she lies in his arms.*] Yes, Vanna,
I understand; I understand your falsehood.
You have achieved the impossible . . . It is
just and very unjust, like all the things that
one does . . . and still it is life that is right
. . . Collect yourself, Vanna; you will have
to lie again, since he refuses to believe . . .
[*Calling* GUIDO.] Guido, she asks for you
. . . Guido, she is coming to herself . . .

GUIDO

[*Rushing up and taking her in his arms.*]
My Vanna! See, she smiles! . . . Vanna,
tell me! . . . I never doubted . . . Now it
is over, and all will be forgotten—wiped away
in our good revenge . . . It was all a bad
dream . . .

VANNA

[*Opening her eyes, and speaking in a
feeble voice.*] Where is he? Yes, yes, I
know, I remember . . . Give me the key
. . . The key of his prison; none but myself
must . . .

GUIDO

The moment the guards come back they
shall bring the key to you, and all shall be as
you wish . . .

VANNA

I want it for myself alone. So that I may
be quite sure, and that no one else . . . Yes,
it has been a bad dream . . . but the beautiful one will begin. The beautiful one will
begin . . .

CURTAIN